Dear Steve,

Mom and I love you as a Son — you are precious to us

God's Servants

Mom Patricia

ISA 41.10

The Morris Cerullo Story

THE CHOSEN WARRIOR

The Morris Cerullo Story

THE CHOSEN WARRIOR

"For many are called, but few are chosen."
Matthew 22:14

MICHAEL WOURMS

FOREWORD BY
PAT BOONE

Creation 🌿 **House**
Lake Mary, Florida

Creation House
Strang Communications Company
600 Rinehart Road
Lake Mary, FL 32746

Unless otherwise noted, all Scripture references are from the King James Version of the Bible.

Scripture references marked NKJV are from the New King James Version of the Bible. Copyright © 1979, 1980, 1982 by Thomas Nelson Inc., Publishers. Used by permission.

Scripture references marked NASB are from the New American Standard Bible copyright 1960, 1962, 1963, 1968, 1971, 1972, 1973, 1975, 1977 by The Lockman Foundation. Used by permission.

DEDICATION

This book is dedicated with loving affection
to Theresa Cerullo, precious wife to Morris Cerullo,
loving mother to David, Mark, and Susan, the first
lady of Morris Cerullo World Evangelism,
and "Mom" to thousands of nationals
around the world.

TABLE OF CONTENTS

FOREWORD

"For many are called, but few are chosen."
Matthew 22:14

Many people are elected, many are appointed, many promoted, many called to fields or positions of endeavor —scientists, corporation presidents, congressmen, military leaders and presidents of nations. They all have one common denominator: an authority that gives them great power with the spoken word or the stroke of a pen.

But few leaders are **chosen** by God. And with that choosing, given a command of God's authority and power that manifests beyond the natural world into an arena of the supernatural.

I have yet to see an authority in this invisible world as powerful as that demonstrated through the ministry of Morris Cerullo. Not by his stature or strength, for he is physically a small man. Not by any power given him by a government, organization, or person. He operates in a supernatural authority bestowed by God.

Using this authority, he has seen God bring to a halt advancing armies, tanks, and even witch doctors, all determined to kill him. He has called on God to stop powers that have held captive and enslaved men, women and children. The exercise of this power has changed the destinies of nations—even nations on the brink of Communist takeover.

Who is this man? A dear friend of mine who lives in Southern California. A man, chosen by God, who could be entrusted to employ so great a power.

This fantastic story of a young Jewish orphan boy will help you to see that, while God does the choosing for specific, ordained assignments, you too can tap into this same power for a dramatic revolution in your personal life and circumstances. **—Pat Boone**

INTRODUCTION

For the past eight years, I've had the distinct privilege of working with and learning from one of the most unusual men on the face of the earth.

As a writer, I am fortunate to come in constant contact with men and women who are household names, national heroes, TV personalities and respected leaders.

But never in my travels have I met anyone with more power and authority to change the course of nations than the gentle giant I call *The Chosen Warrior*.

His story is more exciting than any fiction I could create, any novel that I could fashion to tantalize the reader's fancy.

And even more amazing, all of it is true!

True history often does not emerge until the seasoning of time allows historians to discern which events were significant and which were simply popular.

In the context of his own time, the actions of Abraham Lincoln were not viewed as historically significant. Instead, they were considered by many as divisive to the nation and were greatly criticized.

But in the context of time and history, Lincoln's courageous decisions against slavery have forever exalted his name in history of the United States.

Seldom are nation-changers appreciated or understood in their own time.

Change is always shocking, uncomfortable and threatening.

Lincoln was assassinated.

Ghandi was shot.

Christ was crucified.

It is precisely this historical phenomenon that makes *The Chosen Warrior* remarkable. This book reveals the true story of a man living today who is quietly in the process of impacting the nations of the world.

What an incredible story it makes!

11

"The Chosen Warrior" is a man recognized and loved by millions, has personally spoken to more people than most international politicians, has traveled to over one hundred forty nations. Yet he is barely known in his own country!

As you read this stirring story, I believe you will see, as I did, that we have a rare opportunity to recognize and learn from a man who is affecting the course of history...while that man is still living!

As you read these pages, I am confident that you will agree with me that in the course of modern history, there simply is not another man like him on the face of this earth who has done so much to impact the nations where he has victoriously waged his heated wars without much fanfare or recognition by the national press.

This revealing book will take you on the fascinating journey of this man's life, recount his battles, and reveal the innermost secrets of his strategies for victory.

As you read it, I sincerely believe it will inspire you to change your own life.

For good.

—Michael Wourms

SECTION ONE

FORMED TO FLOURISH

CHAPTER ONE

THE BIRTH OF POWER

It is the greed of the Jews that is causing your economic hardships," the fiery-eyed, black-haired young man sermonized, mesmerizing the crowd with his message.

"Every man should be able to find a job, and every family deserves food on the table...but the only way to make this happen is to take away the economic power from the hands of the Jews."

The rousing speech made this day in 1931 brought hope to a German nation struggling to survive during one of the harshest depressions in its history. Crowds cheered wildly at the inflammatory words of this brash, young political candidate.

Fathers, mothers, families and a hurting nation searching for answers united their voices together as one in support of this young, charismatic leader of the Nationalist Socialist Party.

The solution seemed so simple.

Germany could prosper by merely removing the greedy Jews from all economic power.

And so it was, during this summer day in 1931,

Adolf Hitler thrust himself into the leadership of Germany's largest political party, providing a powerful podium for his meteoric ascendancy to control of Germany and birthing for him an eternal spot in the depraved horror-stories of humanity.

Hitler controlled the day by radiating the extraordinary power of his personality. Single-handedly he dominated the crowds and a desperate nation searching for pride. His charismatic leadership inspired staged spectacles and sparked a new sense of national unity.

That day, Hitler reigned supreme as the leader whose magic animated the masses who assembled to hear him.

His presence dominated the parade and he unceasingly received the adoring salutes from the mechanical marchers passing his podium.

"Never again will the Bolsheviks, or any other nation, ever impose upon Germany the likes of the Versailles Treaty at the close of World War I," he promised his hypnotized supporters.

"And never again will the Jews control our financial destiny."

While this fiery political rhetoric and anti-Jewish poison inspired the Germans, it slowly began to stun the rest of the world.

Many news correspondents that day sent home stories that spoke apprehensively of Germany's growing armed forces and of Hitler's growing belligerent attitude.

"All the talk here has been of peace," wrote one *New York Times* reporter, "yet the atmosphere has been far from peace-loving."

The zeal of Hitler and Nazi Germany on that day in 1931 forged the ideal of Aryan supremacy, an ideal sparked by the smoldering coals of anti-Semitism, fanned by pseudo philosophies, and fired into full flame by the instinctively manipulative hands of the black-haired German leader.

"Today, I want to announce the formation of our Adolf Hitler Nazi Training Schools," he continued, knowing the crowd was totally subject to his iron will. "We will begin to train literally hundreds of thousands of young men between the ages of twelve and eighteen to become perfect German citizens."

The crowd cheered wildly.

Hitler held up his hand for silence.

Immediately, the crowd ceased to breathe.

"The mission of each school will be the same—to *perfect* the German race, to become soldiers trained to wage *total war* against any enemy, and finally...." Here Hitler paused.

He looked intensely at the crowd, first to his left, then to the middle, then to the right. When convinced their minds were affixed anxiously to his final words, he shouted loudly, "...and finally, to eliminate the power, the authority, and the financial control of the Jew from all of Germany."

Those few words soon launched a holocaust of hate unparalleled in the long history of man's inhumanity to man. Eventually, six million Jews would die at the hands of these same Germans who would simultaneously be busy fostering "patriotic pregnancies" to breed their own master race.

But none of this could have been foreseen on that day back in 1931.

The crowd's eyes were blinded by the bright light from their young rising star. Only an insightful few could foresee the human tragedy that would follow in the coming decade.

*　　　*　　　*

A few months after Hitler's prophetic speech, in another part of the world also ravaged by a severe economic depression, on October 2, 1931, a seemingly simple event took place.

There were no *New York Times* reporters on hand to record the incident.

In a quiet neighborhood of Passaic, New Jersey, no one except Mama Bertha, a Russian Orthodox Jew, noticed or much cared about the happening of that day. Without any fanfare or sense of destiny, she proudly brought forth into the world her fifth child, black-haired Moshe (Moses) Cerullo.

No one in Passaic on that October day in 1931 could have possibly sensed any historical significance in that birth.

Mama Bertha did not sense it.

Joseph, the Italian father, would not have sensed the historical significance of the child even if a supernatural lightning bolt blazed a message in front of his house. You see, poor Joseph sat silently in a back room, almost unconscious, in a drunken stupor.

Only the heavens, with bright rays of sunshine piercing the New Jersey clouds, seemed to understand the day. In this one divinely ordained moment a child was born who would have an enormous impact on the history of the Jew and on the eternal destiny of the nations of the world.

CHAPTER TWO

A FOOTBALL
IN THE JUNKYARD
OF LIFE

The young boy instinctively knew something serious had happened.

"Why ya crying, Abe?" Morris asked his older brother.

"Because Mama won't be around to take care of us any more, Morris. She's gone to be with God. Our mama is gone."

Young boys are not very sensitive in their explanations of death. Straight talk, right from the gut.

More tears.

But Abe's words did not fully impact little two-year-old Morris the way they would have shocked an adult. Their significance simply could not sink into his young, inexperienced mind. "Gone" meant she had "gone" to the store, or she had "gone" into another room.

His mama's permanent disappearance from the home simply did not register.

"When is she coming back?" Morris asked, sure this question would settle some of his confusion and put the universe right again.

Abe just put his arm around his little brother and hugged him.

"You've always got your questions, don't ya, little brother? Well, this is one time I can't give you an answer you'll like. Mama's not coming back, little buddy," Abe spoke in a barely audible whisper, "she's not coming back."

Morris strained to grasp the words, but his mind refused to process the finality of Abe's message.

Over the next few weeks, Morris began slowly to understand what it meant for Mama Bertha to be gone. He started to notice small parts of his life changing.

Mama's reassuring hugs disappeared, rudely replaced by the rantings and rages of a drunken dad, whose spirit was ravaged by the hopelessness of the Great Depression and by his wife's death. The unceasing tirades of his father made Morris long even more for his mama's tender touch.

Frances, Pauline, Bernice and Abraham all seemed more serious now. They didn't want to play games much anymore. Oh, they'd play sometimes, but not for very long, and without the frequent laughter that used to make up a part of each day.

"What did I do wrong? Why doesn't anyone like me anymore?" Morris sobbed to himself. His whole world seemed to be changing and he couldn't understand why. Loneliness and anger increasingly became his only childhood companions.

One day, Joseph started drinking even earlier than usual. In an angry, quivering voice, he ordered his five children to "Go into your rooms and put your clothes and shoes into paper bags. You will be staying with someone else for awhile."

And so, with no warning or explanation, another sudden change shook the soul of little Morris.

Later that cold, devastating day, a large black car drove up to the Cerullo household. The driver instructed the five confused children to put their sacks into the trunk and to get in.

They obeyed.

The next few years became a blur of black cars.

Morris learned a new word: "orphanage."

He also learned the meaning of that new word.

"An orphanage is a place where you go and stay for awhile and nobody really cares if you are there or not."

At age four, Morris learned another new word: "foster home."

*   *   *

Roy Hopkins and his wife lived in Teaneck, New Jersey, and were known around the community as decent folks with caring hearts. The Orthodox Jewish junk dealer possessed two acres of old tires, worn-out batteries, piles of brass, iron, and aluminum, and various assorted used car parts.

Old Roy had about everything you'd ever need on that two acres.

Except kids.

When the black car left their house that day, the Hopkins' family increased by five.

And it made sense when you think about it.

Roy spent most his life collecting old, worthless tires. He took those tired tires back to his junkyard, wrapped them in a coat of hot new rubber, put a shiny new tread on them and gave them new life.

Roy Hopkins was in the recycling business.

Old iron was sold to be fired into new car parts. Old batteries, unable to start a car, were cleaned up and given fresh chemicals to spark new life.

Giving new life to worthless waste was his trade, so

it seemed logical that he could work his restoration magic with the Cerullo children.

But balding tires, dead batteries, and rusty hunks of iron do not feel pain, anger, hurt or loneliness. Tires don't mind sitting in a stinky junkyard for two months or two years until someone comes to make them whole.

Children do.

Even at four, Morris knew that moving into the junkyard with Mr. Hopkins was not something that he would brag about to his imaginary friends. Oh no, the junkyard was not the castle of childhood dreams.

Morris felt like an unwanted football in the game of life. Every time someone caught him, they'd kick him, throw him or pound him into the ground. Now Morris felt the game was over, and they'd brought him to the junkyard to rot and die.

*   *   *

"No, I won't do it," the fiery-eyed, defiant five-year-old declared, refusing to apologize for the fight. "He started it in the first place. Called me 'a dirty Jew.' He's the one who should apologize."

The scrappy young man clearly was not intimidated by the school authority standing over him.

"I don't care what you do to me, I won't apologize to that jerk. I hit him once, and if he calls me 'a dirty Jew' again, I'll break his nose."

Morris had simultaneously issued a declaration of war against all Jew-haters and against all authority, knowing full well every ounce of ammunition the opposing arsenals possessed.

"Why you impudent little brat. Sticks and stones will break your bones, but words will never hurt you. You've got to stop fighting every time somebody says something you don't like. Now get into my office this minute. I'll

22

show you who's boss," the principal declared, mistakenly thinking she was in control of this situation.

Morris knew precisely what was coming and fully realized that the opponent had nothing that could possibly penetrate his tough armor.

As often as it was used for this one purpose, the principal's paddle probably should have had the words "For the body of Morris Cerullo, troublemaker" engraved on its flat front. However, for all the good it did, the paddle belonged back in the junkyard with other useless items.

With every whack the young rebel absorbed, his body and mind became more determined, toughened and resistive to the constant challenges of anti-Semitism and authority in his life.

With each whack, he vowed that nothing would break him. Despite the physical pain, Morris showed no visible expression on his face, refusing to let even one single tear to flow from his eyes.

Nothing or no one would ever again make this orphan Jew think he was a worthless football to be kicked around from orphanage to orphanage, from foster home to foster home, from one junkyard to another.

At the early age of five, Morris had instinctively learned how to survive. No foster home, no orphanage, no prejudiced classmate and no school principal was ever again going to determine his value as a person. They could place him in an orphanage, beat him with a paddle, call him 'a dirty Jew' or stick him in a junkyard. It didn't matter.

At five, that decision Morris made would determine the direction of his life. No circumstance or opponent would ever again determine the course of his destiny. No matter what he faced, somehow, some way, he'd overcome the challenge and move on.

By six-and-a-half years of age, the beatings and the rejections became common. After a particularly painful paddling by his principal, Morris defiantly stared at her, then turned and walked away, cursing under his breath.

"You don't have to take this," a small voice inside his throbbing head told him. "It is time to once again run away."

Outside the schoolhouse, in the bright sunlight of day, young Morris started to walk briskly along the nearby railroad tracks as though they were the path to his future. Step by step he followed the tracks right through the local marshes and into the smelly swamps.

He walked quickly, sure that when the principal discovered he was gone she'd organize a search party to bring him home and stick him into a boy's prison. After all, this would be the third time he would appear before a reformatory school board. The two other times he had been returned to the foster home, but he didn't think it would happen again.

The police did pursue Morris, and eventually caught up with him, sitting exhausted on an old sycamore log in the cold mud of the swamp. The warmth of the police car was little solace to a young boy who hated his foster home and school and who didn't want to return to either. He'd rather risk the uncertainty of a night in the wetlands with the wild dogs and snakes than spend another night in the tiny attic bedroom where he slept with his brother and three sisters.

*   *   *

"Thank you, officer," his foster-mother gushed as she gladly greeted the officer and the orphan at the door. "We've been so worried about the little lad," she continued, grabbing Morris firmly by the hair,

24

pulling him roughly inside the house.

Morris knew what was coming next.

As if to affirm his contempt for her authority, Morris yelled at the top of his lungs, "I'll run away again...just as soon as I get another chance."

No sooner did the door slam than his head was yanked down into the cellar where the Cerullo children were forced to eat their meals. The foster-mother took off her shoe and began to beat the boy with the spiked end.

Once.

Twice.

Again and again until his body could no longer stand up under the blows and sunk to the floor.

But his spirit could not be broken.

Sent off to bed without supper, Morris could still be heard cursing underneath his breath, "You can go to hell."

Before the bruises from the beating had healed, Morris once again rode in a black car, this time to a gentile orphanage in Passaic, New Jersey, where he stayed only a few months.

This trip radiated pain.

For the first time, the family unit of brothers and sisters was broken. Abe went into the service, Frances got married and Pauline went to live with friends.

The family was forever fractured and Morris's life was put on hold. The orphanage represented only a temporary holding place until a proper Orthodox Jewish orphanage could be located, where Morris would "be with his own kind."

But the learning process for the orphan kid continued. He discovered how to collect cigarette butts off the dirty streets on his way to school and how to suck a few extra puffs out of them as he hid in the school basement.

This short session of "street smart" education lasted only about sixty days. Soon both Morris and his sister, Bernice, were transferred to their final orphanage, The Daughters of Miriam, in Clifton, New Jersey.

CHAPTER THREE

A PRIMER FOR PREJUDICE, A PATTERN FOR PAIN

In November of 1938, mobs of Nazis smashed the windows of synagogues and stores owned by Jews, leaving the streets and sidewalks littered with glass shards that gave the night its poetic name—Kristallnacht, or Crystal Night.

Nearly one hundred Jews were killed, and thousands more were beaten up and tormented.

Immediately after Crystal Night, twenty thousand well-to-do Jews were arrested. They would be the first of over six million Jews eventually herded into German concentration camps to be tortured, starved, and eventually, shot or gassed.

Hitler publicly proclaimed, "During my struggle for power, the Jews laughed at my prophecies that I would someday assume the leadership of the state. I suppose that the laughing of Jewry is now choking in their throats.

"Today I will be a prophet again.

"If international finance Jewry should succeed once more in plunging the peoples into a world war, then the consequence will not be the Bolshevization of the world and a victory of Jewry, but on the contrary, the destruction of the Jewish race in Europe."

Few understood, at the moment of that odious speech, that Hitler *literally* intended to destroy the entire Jewish race!

In early 1939, the Nazi government started the systematic killing of "worthless and useless" deformed and retarded children. Special "children's centers" in twenty-one hospitals faithfully carried out the killings.

In 1939, the Nazis produced a primer in prejudice, a pattern for pain. Hundreds of thousands of foolish followers throughout the world began to accept the lies. Jews were portrayed in cartoons, in movies and on the radio as bloated, greedy, swarthy, child-molesting, malevolent scoundrels.

In 1939, anti-Semitic campaigns, spearheaded in Germany, began to fan across Europe and wash upon the shores of America, polluting even the neighborhood of The Daughters of Miriam Orphanage with the poison of prejudice.

Jews were likened to rats.

"They carry disease" warned a movie produced in Germany called "The Eternal Jew." Some of the biggest movie houses in the world showed this vile film.

And in 1939, the state of New York placed the Jew, Morris Cerullo, into The Daughers of Miriam Orphanage, where he could be with his own kind of people.

The serene physical setting of the orphanage camouflaged the agony, rejection, frustration, and pain little Morris would continue to experience.

The beautiful green grass on both sides of the main building bid a warm "welcome" to visitors, but to the young child the grass represented a green warning zone that separated the orphanage from the outside world.

28

Instead of "Keep off the Grass," Morris silently thought the sign should read, "Beware of Jews."

The well-maintained ball fields shouted "play ball" to the non-Jewish observer, but Morris knew the ballfields were built because he would not be allowed to "play ball" with the public school kids.

The wooded area behind the orphanage invited exploration and adventure, but the rules and regulations of the orphanage strictly declared that "For your own protection, you are forbidden from wandering off into the woods alone."

On one side of the orphanage sat a picturesque farm that could have been snatched from a Norman Rockwell painting. Morris would soon discover that the word "farm" really meant "work." His primary chore would be to pick the tomatoes.

The young orphan had no real awareness that his older Jewish counterparts, on the other side of the world, were also being separated and orphaned from their families and ordered to provide the physical work force in the concentration camps, so that the Germans could continue to increase their war effort.

Family was important to the Germans and to the Jews. That's why the orphanage was called "Daughters of Miriam." It sounded wholesome and warm, like family.

Yet the younger boys stayed in dormitories, fifteen to a room, in long rows of single beds. "Looks like a damn concentration camp," one of the newer recruits once uttered upon his introduction to the orphanage setting.

One very huge building housed a synagogue, a gym, a dining room and nurse's quarters. Some said it was so the Jews could pray, play, eat and get sick—separate from the rest of New Jersey.

These Jewish orphans lived isolated from society and

separated from each other. Men and boys lived in one wing, women and girls lived in another.

The elderly, abandoned, unwanted Jews lived in a huge, two-story, U-shaped yellow-brick building with a pleasant curved driveway, that made it convenient for their few Saturday visitors to easily come and go.

The Daughters of Miriam radiated a clean, institutional environment and simultaneously represented both separation and solace to those young boys and girls, men and women, and elderly Jews who lived there. These brick buildings were their only protection from the outside atmosphere of prejudice, hatred and pain that was ever-increasing in the Hitler heyday of the late thirties.

*   *   *

"This way, Master Morris," Rabbi Gold instructed, leading the young boy down the hall. "I understand you can be quite a problem. Well, I think we've come up with a few solutions to your shenanigans. To help you stop getting into so many fights, I've decided to put you in with the older boys. Don't think you'll give them quite the guff you're used to dishing out."

Morris followed, not saying a word.

Rabbi Gold continued.

"Of course, you'll be expected to follow all the rules and to pitch in with the chores. You'll have a shift at washing dishes...you'll clean fish on Fridays...and you look strong enough," Rabbi Gold said, feeling the start of a muscle on Morris's arm before he had a chance to pull away, "so you will learn how to run the potato peeling machine. You'll also be expected to...."

As the rabbi continued to recite the endless litany of rules and regulations, Morris's mind drifted off in more sinister directions, already sizing up the vulnerability of the institution, noticing locks, unlatched windows and anything tempting he might steal.

*   *   **

The white handkerchief pressed against his face could not hide the evidence. Morris had just returned from the public school he attended and from one of his frequent after-school fights.

"Another bloody nose at school today, Master Morris?" asked Rabbi Gold, shaking his head. "When are you ever going to stop this nonsense?"

"When they stop calling me a kike," Morris snapped, trying to sound brave and tough, but inwardly worn by the constant degradation and isolation each day seemed to bring. "What's the use of fighting anymore," Morris thought as his nose throbbed in pain. "What's the use of fighting anymore. I hit one guy, and another pops up. I can't beat them all. There's just too many of them, and there's only one of me. And I'm getting awful tired."

Morris jolted from his depressive thoughts at the familiar voice of Rabbi Gold.

"Well, go get some ice out of the kitchen and put it on that thing before it swells up twice as big," the rabbi said, smiling a bit and sounding as compassionate as Morris had ever heard him. "But hurry up though," he quickly added, as if to reassert his authority, "Torah class is in ten minutes."

"Who cares about that damn class anyway," Morris thought to himself. "It's like learning about the history of a junkyard. The only one proud of it is the junkyard owner. I hate being a Jew," Morris thought with every throb of his nose.

As he continued down the hallway, another young orphan named Joey, totally unaware of the raging fire now burning almost out of control in Morris, made a remark he would instantly regret.

31

"Well, Morris, looks like they got the best of you in school today."

Morris erupted.

Instantly, and before Joey could throw a punch, he was flat on the floor facing a flurry of flying fists.

Once.

Twice.

Again and again Morris pummeled the poor boy. Finally, in one final thrust, he hit Joey's face so hard that it bounced back up off the floor, his forehead plowing into Morris's mouth, chipping one of Morris's teeth.

"My God," yelled Rabbi Gold upon catching the last part of this violent scene, "I do believe you've gone crazy." He ran over and pulled the possessed young man off the confused and hurting Joey.

Morris had to be restrained for several minutes by Rabbi Gold before he finally calmed down. "I'll kill 'em, I'll kill 'em, I'll kill 'em," he kept shouting in a rage that clearly was not intended for just Joey.

When the blood from the nose had stopped and the rage from his soul had subsided, they took Morris to the hospital for emergency care to his tooth. Eventually, the tooth would be capped, but there was no earthly doctor available who could cap the anger, the rage and the pain still throbbing inside the body of that little orphan.

Joey never said another careless word to Morris "Madman" Cerullo.

That night, while in bed, but not able to sleep, Morris wept bitterly.

"It just isn't gonna stop," he sobbed to himself. "I can't take it any more. I'm sick of the fighting. My nose hurts. My tooth aches. My heart hurts. I just can't take it anymore. I hate being a Jew and an orphan."

Morris finally stopped crying. He decided at that

moment that there was a perfect, permanent solution to his pain.

The young eight-year-old quietly got up from his bed, and slowly walked down the long hallway to the bathroom. He noticed the hallway clock said 2:00 a.m.

As he entered the bathroom, Morris methodically checked to make sure no one followed him. He then walked over to the bathroom window and stood silently, staring out from the second story.

For the last six years he'd been without a mother, had seen his drunken father only two times, and was now separated from all of his family except one sister. This alienation from his family, his schoolmates, and from society had finally taken its devastating toll on the young man's seemingly indomitable spirit.

On this night, when other children dreamed of fairy tale worlds and sand castle kingdoms, Morris plotted his suicide.

Slowly he slid the wooden-framed window up and climbed out on the cold ledge, looking at the hard and unyielding concrete down below.

"All I need to do is just jump off and it will all be over," thought young Morris, honestly wanting this quick action to end the pain in his heart.

He jumped a bit when he heard a cricket announcing the lateness of the evening.

Morris got into a crouch, poising himself to leap once and for all away from the frustrations, the angers, the isolation and the hurt of this life.

In just a few seconds it would all be over.

He took one last deep breath, and it seemed like his heart stopped beating. For an instant, the entire universe stopped, suddenly silent and still, waiting to watch the final seconds of this young eight-year-old boy's life.

"Who's that," Morris whispered, suddenly aware of the presence of another being.

He slowly and carefully turned and looked back into the washroom to see who would try and stop his leap.

The washroom was empty.

Yet, Morris knew he was not alone.

In a solitary instant, the entire evening suddenly radiated a peace that surpassed all his youthful understanding. He looked down, then finally, upward at the beautiful stars and moon with all their brightness and glory.

"My God, what a beautiful sight," he thought to himself, actually suspended in time, physically paralyzed by the serene and overwhelmingly beautiful scene in the heavens.

At that moment, Morris experienced a peculiar sensation from the crown of his head to the soles of his feet. It rocketed through his unmoving body, painlessly burning out all the unwanted feelings and emotions along the way.

Suddenly, his nose stopped hurting.

His tooth stopped throbbing.

His heart stopped aching.

His very soul now seemed strangely cleansed and calm.

His anger ceased.

At a time in history when millions of innocent Jews were about to be slaughtered in far away Germany, somehow, for some reason unknown to this tiny little orphan Jew, a powerful presence from a heavenly source intervened and preserved his life.

Morris, the orphan, instinctively knew that in this vast universe he was no longer alone.

Morris Cerullo knew someone, somewhere, cared very deeply about him!

Unconsciously, he climbed back inside the safety of the washroom, his eyes still fixed upward, his heart greatly calmed by the supernatural presence.

The anger, the distress, the despondency that drove him down the hall that night had dissipated.

Morris noticed the hall clock now read 2:45 a.m. as he floated back to his bed, peaceful for the first time in six years.

Somehow, in forty-five minutes that had seemed to zip past as forty-five seconds, the life of Morris Cerullo would never be the same.

CHAPTER FOUR

CHILD
OF THE LAKE

Many of you soon will be experiencing Bar Mitzvah, one of the most sacred events of your
Jewish heritage," Rabbi Gold declared to the
small group of Jewish boys who sat listening to his
teaching.

"Bar Mitzvah means 'son of the commandment,' and
is intended to remind you that our Jewish law assumes
a child is a religiously responsible adult at the age of
thirteen plus one day."

For once, Morris did not mind being in class. The
strange, yet somehow sacred events of the night before
on that window ledge eased his resentment for Jewish
history, and replaced it with an incomprehensible
peace—and yes, even a sense of inquisitiveness towards
his heritage.

Rabbi Gold continued.

"Now, since one of the privileges of the Jewish adult
is being called upon to read the Torah, the first Torah-
reading service after you reach thirteen is an important
occasion. It is the first time you can publicly declare your
allegiance to the Torah. Unfortunately, in this day and

age, Bar Mitzvah has mainly come to be associated with festivities and fun."

At that remark, the entire group of Jewish orphans all cheered wildly. Even Morris laughed as he thought to himself, "Maybe something good can come from this Bar Mitzvah stuff yet!"

"Rabbi Gold," one of the students asked respectfully, "where is Bar Mitzvah mentioned in the Torah?"

"It isn't," Rabbi Gold replied. "Jewish historians trace the Bar Mitzvah ceremony back about four hundred to six hundred years. But just because it is not mentioned in the Torah does not make it not so. Did you know that the Ten Commandments are never called that in the Bible or in Hebrew! In fact, there aren't and never were *ten* commandments."

"Ah, come on," one of the more pessimistic young minds objected, "everybody knows there are ten commandments."

"Not so," Rabbi Gold continued confidently. "The first of this group of laws is not stated as a command, but as an assertion of fact: 'I am the Lord Thy God.' What follows is a series of moral precepts, not commandments. In rabbinic literature, the entire group is called Asereth Hadibroth, which means 'ten sayings.' The Bible itself, in Deuteronomy 4:13 and 10:4, refers to them not as Ten Commandments but as Asereth Hadevarim, or 'ten words.' "

Today, instead of finding this class boring and tedious, Morris noticed something unusual happening. He actually was interested in what Rabbi Gold was saying about the Torah. He picked up his pencil and started to take notes.

Rabbi Gold noticed the change in Morris as he continued to teach.

"And I'll tell you another thing that's interesting. For

example, Mr. Morris, did you know that your own name, *Moses*, is not technically Hebraic?''

"No sir," Morris replied, surprised at his own respectfulness.

"That's right. It's derived from the language of Israel's ancient enemy, Egypt. 'Moses' is Egyptian for 'Child of the Lake,' and this was the name given by the Pharoah's daughter to the baby she spotted in a cradle floating in the Nile.''

"How similar we were," Morris thought to himself. "Moses lost his real mom, and so did I. Moses was put in a basket and shipped from one place to another. Instead of a basket, I got a black car.''

"What about the word 'Jew,' Rabbi Gold, where does that come from?'' one of the elder students asked, snapping Morris back to attention.

"That's a good question," the Rabbi answered, never stumped by their challenges. "The term 'Jew' does not appear in the five books of Moses and is used for the first time in the Book of Esther, which tells of the persecution of the Jews in Persia around twenty-three hundred years ago. The word 'Jew' evolved from the name of Jacob's son, Judah, which means 'to praise God.' ''

"Yeah, that's what it meant then," one of the more hardened orphans complained, "but today it just means you are scum or someone to make fun of and use as a punching bag.''

A single chorus of "yeahs" went up in the classroom. Not one young man sitting in that classroom had escaped the now anti-Semitic movement sweeping across the world.

Rabbi Gold couldn't help but notice that today was one of those rare classes when the student's interest was actually perked to a peak of enthusiastic participation.

"How about Jerusalem? What does that mean, Rabbi Gold?" another student asked.

"Jerusalem means 'City of Peace,'" the seasoned teacher responded, "but ironically it has been ruled by fourteen different peoples."

He recited the next two sentences without even glancing at his notes.

"The Canaanites, Israelites, Egyptians, Assyrians, Babylonians, Persians, Greeks, Romans, Byzantines, Saracens, Arabs, the Crusaders, Ottoman Turks and the British. Miraculously, through all these conquests, from the time the Jews entered the Promised Land, Jerusalem has never lost its Jewish associations."

Now it was Morris's turn to ask a question.

"Why is there so much hatred for us today?"

"That's a complicated question, Master Morris," Rabbi Gold responded. "The Jewish race has been hated almost since the beginning of time. Even today, the Germans who yell so loudly that we are the source of all evil really owe the settlement of their land to Jews. The Jews lived in Germany before the Germans did!"

"Is that really true, Rabbi Gold?" another student asked.

"Yes, the Jews lived in Germany before the destruction of the Second Temple. In the beginning of the fourth century, they had an organized community in Cologne, with a synagogue, lay leaders and, of course, rabbis. The rights of this Jewish enclave were laid down in an edict by the Emperor Constantine in the year 321 A.D. Not until later did the Teutons cross the Rhine and settle in the old Roman province. Until then, a person could be better understood in Cologne if he spoke Hebrew rather than German!"

The class erupted in a unified expression of delight.

Suddenly, they were very proud of their heritage.

"And that's not all," Rabbi Gold continued hurriedly, not wanting to lose the magic of this moment. "Although we only make up one percent of Germany's population, we have sixteen percent of the practicing lawyers, ten percent of the doctors and dentists, and seventeen percent of the bankers!"

Again, cheers exploded in the classroom.

Rabbi Gold smiled proudly.

At least on this one day he knew his knowledge was getting through to his young minds.

"Be proud of your Jewishness," he instructed them. "When this great country was founded, Benjamin Franklin, John Adams and Thomas Jefferson knew Jewish history so well that they wanted the seal of the United States to depict the Israelites escaping from Egypt."

The class cheered again.

"And that's not all," Rabbi Gold hastened to continue, now caught up in the excitement of the moment. "Did you know that the very inscription on our Liberty Bell, 'Proclaim liberty throughout all the land unto all inhabitants thereof,' comes from the Jewish Bible?

"That's right," he continued, not waiting for their answer. "It's in Leviticus 25:10, in reference to the ancient Israelites' celebration of the jubilee, the fifty-year anniversary when the land was allowed to lie fallow, debts were forgiven, slaves were freed, and everyone began anew."

Cheers, clapping, and frenzy.

Rabbi Gold hadn't played baseball since he was a boy, but on this day he felt as though he'd just hit a home run!

For a few meaningful moments of temporary escape from the real world, being a Jew did not seem so bad to these now cheering young men.

41

Morris's mind began to wander at the rabbi's last words.

Forgiven.

Freed.

Begin anew.

They sounded so familiar and comforting.

Those very words perfectly described the feeling of his own supernatural experience from the night before.

"Maybe the God of Israel is telling me that that this is my time of jubilee," Morris thought, writing down the words "Leviticus 25:10" in his notebook.

CHAPTER FIVE

STORM
BEFORE THE CALM

Ever since she got religion at that Baptist revival meeting," her husband claimed, "she's just not the same woman I married."

And he was right.

When Ethel Kerr started to serve God, her marriage became a daily arena of unceasing conflict. She wanted to place her family under God's biblical standards and Mr. Kerr demanded to keep things "just the way they are."

Marital disagreements in the Kerr household became increasingly frequent and volatile.

"How the hell can you talk to God?" Ethel's confused husband shouted as he banged the table with his fist. "I've never heard of such nonsense. Ethel, I don't know what's happened to you, but you've changed. You know that? You've changed."

"If you'd just let me pray with you," the lovely young wife patiently replied, "you will begin to feel what I feel, to know what I am learning, to understand how God can guide our lives. I don't hear Him in an audible voice, but I know when He's talking to me, and I know He hears my prayers."

"You've really gone over the edge, Ethel," her husband sighed, throwing up his hands and walking out of the room. "I give up. I just give up. I can't even talk to you anymore," she could hear him say as he slammed the front door on his way out into the night.

After what seemed like an eternity of these non-productive marital conflicts and after exhausting every other possibility, Ethel Kerr was finally forced to leave her husband, her two children and her secure home to start a new life.

Alone.

She left home with only a few dollars and the clothes on her back and her precious Bible.

She immediately began to look for steady work to support herself. Many a day Ethel walked the dirty streets between job interviews, desperately looking for lost dimes and nickles in the gutters to buy herself a cup of soup or a loaf of stale, day-old bread.

Years ago, she had worked as a practical nurse.

"Perhaps I can get another job in the nursing field," she mused as she bought a newspaper with the bold, black heading, "Hitler's Troops Invade Soviet Union."

Indeed, World War II was escalating, but Ethel Kerr hardly noticed. Every day she fought her own private war just to survive, waging battle after battle against invisible enemies like hunger, loneliness and despair.

For the next few difficult and frustrating years, Ethel struggled through job after job, living with one constantly nagging question. "Lord," she asked repeatedly, "how is this life I'm living going to make any difference in your vast, eternal plan?"

One night, after a particularly long and demanding day, Ethel's spirit sunk into deep despair when she came home from work. "Lord, let me die," she cried tearfully. "Take me home to You. I can't stand this life any longer. What are you waiting for? Take me home to be with You."

After this tragic prayer of utter desperation, she slouched down in the one small chair in her barren apartment and grabbed a magazine up off the floor. She began to flip through the pages when her eyes noticed this poem by Ira Sankey.

She began to read:

Not now, my child, a little more rough tossing,
A little longer on the billows foam:
A few more journeyings in the desert darkness,
And then the sunshine of thy Father's home.
Not now, for I have wanderers in the distance,
And thou must call them in with patient love:
Not now, for I have loved ones sad and weary,
Wilt thou not cheer them with a kindly smile?
Sick ones who need thee in their lonely sorrow,
Wilt thou not tend them yet a little while?
Not now, for wounded hearts are sorely bleeding,
And thou must teach those widowed hearts to sing:
Not now, for orphan's tears are quickly falling,
They must be gathered 'neath some sheltering
* wing"*
(emphasis added).

There was more to the poem, but the "not now" message rang so loudly in her heart that it felt like a man with a hammer in his hand was banging the Liberty Bell right there in her small living room.

Another single tear carefully made its way down her pretty cheek. "Yes, Lord," she whispered, "I do understand. "Someday I will be with You in heaven, but 'not now.' You still have a job for me to do.

"Oh God, I beg Your forgiveness for my impatience

45

in serving you," she continued, "and for my cowardly despair. Lord, I stand willing to obey Your will and do as You direct. Amen."

As she prayed, her mind suddenly remembered a strange scripture which she had come across in her Bible study only a few days before. She had felt then that the message was for her, but didn't understand what it meant:

"Take counsel, execute judgment; make thy shadow as the night in the midst of the noonday; hide the outcasts; bewray not him that wandereth. *Let mine outcasts dwell with thee*" (Isaiah 16:3-4; emphasis added).

"That's it," she thought to herself. "God knows that I'm living as an outcast and now I'm being directed to reach out to society's outcasts, the orphans."

Her small part in a larger supernatural plan now seemed much much clearer.

A few days later, in another time of prayer, Ethel noticed a special scripture for her further specific guidance.

"...be not afraid of them neither be afraid of their words, though briers and thorns *be* with thee, and thou dost dwell among scorpions: be not afraid of their words, nor be dismayed at their looks, though they *be* a rebellious house....But thou...hear what I say unto thee; Be not thou rebellious like that rebellious house: open thy mouth, and eat that I give thee....*Get thee unto the house of Israel and speak with my words unto them. For thou* art *not sent to a people of a strange speech and of an hard language,* but *to the house of Israel*" (Ezekiel 2:6-3:5, passim; emphasis added).

Until that moment, Ethel had felt in her heart that God wanted her to go to a foreign country as a missionary. But with this scripture, she now knew differently.

"How can I be a missionary if God is not calling me to a land with 'strange speech,'" she reasoned. "It seems my Lord wants me to stay here in America and minister to the 'house of Israel,' the Jews in my own land who speak my own language."

After years of patient and difficult waiting, after years of wandering in the uncertain wilderness of jobs and provision, God's plan for her life now seemed clearer. Like the Jews of old who had fled from Egypt, she had spent her time in the desert, and now God was ready to lead her to the Promised Land!

A few weeks later, Ethel received a letter from the president of the Hebrew Christian Synagogue.

"Dear Mrs. Kerr,

As you know, the Hebrew Christian Synagogue has a major outreach to the Jews here in New York City. Today, I would like to formally offer you a position as a full-time worker on my staff. I believe you will be of great assistance in our outreach to the Jews. Hope to see you soon in New York."

Ethel held the letter lightly in her palms as if she were holding a sacred document written by the very hand of God. This seemed to be heaven itself opening up to her!

Without a moment's hesitation, she immediately gave notice to her employer of just a few weeks and made the necessary preparations to go to New York. At last, God's plan for her life was coming to pass.

How exciting it would be to work full-time with God's chosen people, the Jews! The difficult years of hardship, loneliness, worry and self-sacrifice had at last all been worth it.

The next few weeks seemed like months, but finally, the time arrived when she would take the train for New York. Alone in her room the night before she was to leave, a most peculiar sensation came over her.

Ethel felt sick all over her body.

Strength began to drain from her arms and legs.

"Oh God, please don't let me become sick now," she cried out into the darkness of her room. "You know I must go to New York tomorrow to begin my work for Thee. Please help me."

In this passionate prayer, God spoke to her spirit words she did not understand. "My servant, if you will obey, I will heal you. Do not go to New York."

Ethel could not believe the sudden turn of events.

"But Lord, the door is open," Ethel replied, dumbfounded by the order. "You have made the way for me."

"If you will obey me and not go," God answered, "I will heal you of this sickness by morning."

Ethel, confused and distressed by this bizarre shift in direction, nevertheless vowed to obey God.

She slipped into bed and slept quietly all night. The next morning, she woke perfectly refreshed.

All her signs of sickness had disappeared.

Since there were only a few dollars left out of her final pay from her last job, she got a morning newspaper and once again began the arduous process of answering the "help-wanted" ads. She journeyed to one interview, then another, frequently having the door closed right in her face.

One night, she went back to her room, tired and discouraged, and cried out from her heart, "Oh Lord, what shall I do? I have obeyed You. What shall I do now? You must help me."

After praying, she wearily collapsed into her chair and glanced through the newspaper again, noticing an ad she'd somehow neglected to see before. It read:

"Daughters of Miriam Orphanage, Old People's Home. Practical nurse wanted."

Those words seemed to jump right out of the page. The more she tried to disregard those words, the more they kept jumping out at her. "Lord, this advertisement is referring to a Jewish Home, can't You read?"

Then, as if in a slight rebuke, God spoke to her spirit and said, "I can read. Can't you hear? I want you to answer this advertisement. I will go before you. I will make a way where there is no way. I have spoken and I shall bring it to pass."

CHAPTER SIX

LIGHT UNDER THE COVERS

It was 1:57 a.m.

The entire orphanage was peacefully sleeping, except for two mischievous teenage boys who quietly made their way from their beds through the long, narrow corridor.

"God, is this exciting," one whispered a bit too loudly.

"Shut up," Morris snapped. "We don't want anyone to hear us."

The two young men gingerly tiptoed down the flight of stairs leading to the first floor. Their hearts were beating so fast and so loudly that Morris wondered how those sleeping could not hear the noise.

Finally, the two young men stood at the end of another long corridor which led to the orphanage office where the safe was kept.

Like two professional thieves, they carefully and quietly opened up the office door, which offered only one tiny squeak of protest.

Immediately, they entered the room and walked straight to the old iron safe in the corner.

Morris took out a flat metal object and began to pry

at the safe door. He put all of his shoulder weight behind the metal bar, using the best leverage he could, but to no avail.

The safe door would not budge.

"Damn," the two boys said simultaneously. "I didn't think this old thing would be that strong," Morris whispered. "Guess we'll have to look somewhere else for our money."

"Hey, what about the petty cash box?" the other boy suggested. "There's always something in there."

With a quick change in plans, the two would-be-thieves quietly hurried over to the desk drawer where the petty cash box was kept. Morris knew right where it was located since he'd often seen Rabbi Gold fetch it to pay for the deliveries of ice for the icebox.

Inch by inch, as if uncovering a sacred treasure, the two villains slowly slipped open the cash box. There they were—several crisp dollar bills just sitting there, waiting to be spent!

They took out every bill in the box and silently made their way out of the office, shut the squeaky door and headed down to the cellar where they could safely count their booty.

"Morris, this is great. I can't believe we got away with it," the younger accomplice said in a high-toned, excited whisper. "But how do we get out of here to spend it?"

"Why that's no problem," Morris replied very calmly, with a cocky, arrogant tone in his voice. "When you've been here as long as I have, you know these things."

Morris, the burglar, now became Morris, the carpenter, electrician, and escape artist.

Carefully, Morris removed the wooden baseboard from the wall, exposing a long electric line.

"This wire connects with the main alarm system,"

Morris explained to his junior partner in crime. "All we have to do is disconnect these two wires right here, and presto, we are free."

Back in the forties, alarm systems were not as sophisticated as they are today. Who knows, perhaps clever young thieves like Morris inspired some inventor to create an alarm system that activates whenever there's a break in the line. But for tonight, no such system existed, and so Morris and his admiring friend were now free to leave the orphanage without any alarms announcing their exit.

Sneaking out the orphanage front door, the two delinquents enjoyed a night of freedom and fun, buying cigarettes, drinking alcohol, and spending every last dollar bill they had stolen.

At 7:17 a.m., Rabbi Gold walked into his office and discovered the robbery. Upstairs, Master Morris and his friend were just getting out of bed, pretending, in the best tradition of amateur actors, that they had just completed a marvelous night's sleep.

*　　　*　　　*

"Right this way, Mrs. Kerr." Rabbi Gold motioned for the young lady to take the seat across from his desk. "I apologize for all the confusion around here. Had a robbery last night. Nothing much lost. Just some money from our cash box. Won't you come in?"

"Thank you, Rabbi Gold," she replied, hoping he would not notice the frayed edges of her dress.

"Kerrrrr," Rabbi Gold said slowly. "That doesn't sound Jewish," Rabbi Gold observed, asking a question without really asking it.

"That's because it isn't Jewish," Mrs. Kerr responded. "Unless I misread the ad, Rabbi Gold, I'm here for the position of practical nurse, not for the position of rabbi."

"Oh yes, of course, of course. Excellent point," the administrator chuckled. For the better part of the next forty-five minutes, Rabbi Gold fired a series of questions at Mrs. Kerr to confirm the decision he had already made after her first quick-witted, confident comeback to his subtle question about her Jewishness.

Within twenty-four hours after the interview, Mrs. Kerr, Christian nurse, had moved into the nurses' quarters of the Daughters of Miriam Jewish Orphanage.

She wondered which Jewish member of the board of directors, which Jewish administrator, or perhaps which elderly Jewish lady would be the target of her first missionary witness for God's glory.

Not once did it enter her mind to think of one of those little ones. After all, God would not bring her this far to witness to one little boy or girl.

After several months at the orphanage, doing her daily chores without even a single chance to witness the message of Jesus Christ to those around her, Mrs. Kerr found herself getting tired and discouraged.

"Oh God," she prayed, "I know you didn't just bring me here to make the beds of old people. I have been here many months already and I have not had one chance to testify or witness for You. I know You sent me here. Please, just show me the reason why, or speak to me, and I shall be satisfied."

God heard the cry of this impatient servant, and lovingly spoke these words into her spirit: "My daughter, look yonder to the pathway."

Rushing over to the window, the excited nurse noticed a concrete driveway that went all around one side of the orphanage.

Coming up the walk was a wayward orphan boy.

God spoke to His missionary messenger again.

"When that boy was eight years old, I heard a cry from his heart. I saw something which I could get hold of and use for My honor and glory. I purposed that day to bring My message to him. That boy is the reason why I have led you here."

Mrs. Kerr shivered and felt goosebumps on her arms as she turned away from the window after the young boy drifted out of sight.

She felt strange.

Nervous.

Excited.

Sick.

Her throat felt like dry chalk.

Her quivering knees could barely support her.

She stood absolutely motionless for several seconds while her eyes went heavenward. "Oh God, I thank you," she whispered in a voice of reverence, humbly rejoicing in the Lord's answer to her prayer. "How I thank You!"

Mrs. Kerr finally resumed the once tedious task of making the bed, only this time joy exploded in her heart. While humming one of her favorite tunes, "Amazing Grace," she silently vowed to God that she would continue making beds and changing dressings for His glory until she could witness to that young man, even if it took the rest of her life!

*   *   *

"Morris, I want to talk to you for a few minutes," the nurse said as she approached the unsuspecting young man.

"Yes, ma'am," Morris replied respectfully, knowing full well that although he hated all authority, he also understood the easiest way to play their games.

"I have something special for you, Morris," she

continued, tentatively holding out a five-cent candy bar towards him.

Anger instantly raged in the young man.

Alarm systems immediately activated in this young man's street-wise head. He had lived too long to be fooled by anyone! This lady wanted something, and he wasn't about to give it.

To display his independence and his disdain for her suspicious actions, Morris took the candy bar from Mrs. Kerr and threw it violently to the ground!

"I don't want any of your stupid candy," he said. "Just leave me alone," he snapped.

Before Mrs. Kerr knew or understood what had just happened, Morris was gone.

"Who does she think she is? What does she think she is doing?" Morris fumed to himself as he hurried to pick tomatoes on the orphanage farm. "I don't need her or anyone else to be nice to me. If I want a candy bar, I'll steal the money and buy my own."

But Mrs. Kerr did not get discouraged.

The next time Morris passed her, she smiled broadly at the lad and said "Hello, Morris" as if the candy bar incident never happened.

Many more times in the next few weeks they met and each time Mrs. Kerr had a big smile for Morris. She was always very nice to the hostile teenager.

Weeks turned into months, and Mrs. Kerr's kindness was finally more than Morris could take. The smiles had worn down his callous exterior and sharpened his insatiable curiosity.

"I'm going to go to that woman and find out what she is up to," Morris finally decided, determined to unlock the mystery of her friendliness.

Late one night, well past midnight, when Morris was

sure no one would run a bed check in his room, he slipped down the fire escape into the dark night. He walked about the back court a while, reassuring himself that no one saw him leave his room.

Next, he snuck over to the nurses' quarters—a special wing of the building for all the nurses and hired help. The door leading into that section of the building was locked.

"Damn," Morris exclaimed to himself, not expecting this development. As he searched for a solution, he thought, "Maybe I can scale that wall over there. It ends up right under Mrs. Kerr's window."

Slowly and cautiously he climbed on the crevices in the wall until he was about ten feet off the ground, right next to Mrs. Kerr's window. Quickly, he grabbed the safety of the window sill, and then climbed up on it.

"Six years ago I stood on a window sill just like this wanting to kill myself," he thought. "Now the last thing I want to do is die."

Morris knocked on Mrs. Kerr's window.

Once.

Twice.

A third time.

No one responded.

"Surely," Morris thought, "she must be in her room at this late hour."

On the inside of her room, Mrs. Kerr was almost having a heart attack! "Who or what is that?" she thought to herself in a state of nervous panic. "Could it be an angel?" she questioned, then answered her own query. "Oh no, of course not, a little thing like a window would never stop one of God's messengers."

No.

It had to be a human.

Finally, she mustered up enough courage to go over to the window and peek. When she saw Morris, she was thrilled, elated and relieved. She immediately opened the window wide, grabbed his hand, and helped him inside.

"Why, Morris, what in tarnation brings you here at this time of night?" she asked, secretly knowing in her heart the answer.

"Because..." he hesitated, not sure how to phrase it. "Because I want to know why you are being so nice to me."

"Well, Morris," Mrs. Kerr replied in her softest voice, "have a seat and we will talk about it."

Thus began one of the most exciting discourses in Morris's life. Oh yes, at first Morris threw his cynical darts and asked pessimistic questions, but Mrs. Kerr always had the same smile, the same soft answer, the same restful and quiet spirit.

That night marked the first of many similar conversations. Morris would come to visit Mrs. Kerr over and over again. These secret evening conversations covered a myriad of interesting topics.

They talked about the heroes of faith in the Old Testament. Morris had studied the lives of these men before in Hebrew school. At the age of thirteen, he had his Bar Mitzvah and participated in other Jewish ceremonies and feast days, including Passover and the Day of Atonement.

They talked about Moses, Abraham, Isaac, Jacob, David, Samuel and other Old Testament characters. Yet, the Moses Mrs. Kerr spoke about was a new Moses to Morris. He wasn't just Jewish. He became alive as a man of God, full of love and meekness.

Abraham was not just a wanderer, but a man who "...looked for a city which hath foundations, whose builder and maker is God."

Elijah, Elisha, the prophets all came alive through Mrs. Kerr's words as men who longed to do the will of God. They knew the reality of a God of the living, who is ever present to help them in their time of need.

"Mrs. Kerr," Morris asked one evening, "do you think it was actually God watching out for me that night when I was going to take my own life? Do you think He really watches over each of us that personally?"

"Yes, Morris," Mrs. Kerr explained, sharing with him what God told her that day when she saw him walking down the driveway. "I know God was watching out for you when you were eight, just like He is watching out for you today."

Without being fully aware of it, Morris's heart and life began to change.

He stopped thinking about stealing.

The cold, outward veneer was slowing being melted.

He stopped smoking and cursing.

One day, because she knew it was Morris's ambition as a young man to become a lawyer and because she respected his extremely inquisitive mind, Mrs. Kerr presented him with a tract called "Questions." It was written by James Bennett, a Christian lawyer. This time, unlike the candy bar, Morris did not throw the tract on the ground. Instead, he took it to his room and read it.

Devoured it.

After that, Morris put so many questions to Mrs. Kerr that she could not possibly answer them without supernatural knowledge from God—so keen was his mind.

One evening, after another of their secret studies, Mrs. Kerr said, "Morris, it is too dangerous for you to be coming to my room all the time. Eventually, someone is going to see you."

As she spoke, she took a little black book from her

pocket. "This is a gift for you. Now you don't have to take it if you don't want to," she said, still aware that Morris was always skeptical of kindness, "but I have a little book here I would like you to have. It's a Pocket New Testament. Would you care to read it for yourself?"

"Why sure," he responded, surprised his friend was still so cautious. "Of course I'd like to have it." By this time, Morris was anxious to get his hands on anything that would teach him more about this new way of life.

"Here's something else you'll need," Mrs. Kerr said, handing her eager pupil a little pen flashlight. "The only time you'll be able to read this New Testament is at night, when everybody else is sleeping. And remember, be very, very careful. If you ever get caught reading the New Testament, it would be very hard for you."

"Ah, I'm not afraid," Morris instinctively replied, trying to cover up his boyish fear. "But they won't ever catch me. I'm too clever for them," he told her, "so don't you worry none."

After "lights out," at about eleven o'clock the next evening, Morris took out his New Testament, pulled the covers of his bed over his head, turned on the pen flashlight, and began to read.

First one page, then another, and another.

One chapter, then another.

One book, then another.

He read and read until he had completed the first four Books—Matthew, Mark, Luke and John.

Never before had he read anything more wonderful!

This book revealed a man, misunderstood, beaten, laughed at, scourged, ridiculed, persecuted, mocked beyond degree, and yet there was something of purpose in His actions. He came into this world, was not of this world, but He could have had this world.

The only doctrine Morris had ever learned was "an eye for an eye and a tooth for a tooth." He thought the first one to get in the first punch was the one who came up the victor in any conflict.

But this man's teachings and His whole life were contrary to anything Morris had ever seen or heard!

Here was a man who taught men to love one another, to do good and to hate evil. He had no clothes but the clothes on His back. No purse of riches, but the fruit of His influence on the lives of men and women. He possessed a wooden cross instead of the golden riches of this world, that could have been His.

Here was a man whose kingdom was not of clay, hay, wood or stubble, but was the hearts of humanity. His riches were their love and devotion.

Jesus Christ was the Son of God!

He read on and on.

About other great men.

Peter.

Paul.

John.

"Oh my," he thought, "how they must have loved this Jesus Christ to live for Him, suffer for Him, and even die for Him."

Morris read until he could not keep his eyes open any longer.

His heart hungered. And here was the Bread of Life!

His mind was thirsty. And here was the Fountain of Living Waters!

Each night, Morris read and read. When he finished, he would cautiously hide his New Testament and pen flashlight between the mattress and spring of the bed.

And sometimes, in the quiet of day, Morris and Mrs. Kerr would sneak in conversations about the mysteries unfolding in this young man's life.

Mrs. Kerr had been attending fine denominational churches for her own personal worship, but one day she was invited to what people call a "Pentecostal church." Pentecostal churches preach the same Christ, the same salvation, the same separated life as other Christian churches, but they also believe one other doctrine called "the baptism of the Holy Spirit."

After attending this Pentecostal service, Mrs. Kerr came back all excited, telling Morris, "The special characteristic of their meetings," she said, "is praising the Lord aloud and all praying together. Oh Morris, God felt so real during this service. Here, take this," she said, handing him a magazine called *The Pentecostal Evangel*. "It will help you understand what I'm talking about."

Morris gladly took the magazine. By now, he wanted anything that would satisfy his hungry heart and searching mind.

After the last room check that evening, he took his new magazine in to the washroom and read it under the light by the mirror. After he finished, he put the magazine in his bathrobe pocket and returned to his room where he removed the bathrobe and hung it on the locker.

The next morning, the orphanage administration decided to hold a locker inspection of the beds and rooms. Another nurse, who was checking the boy's dormitory, opened Morris's locker. There, protruding from the pocket of the bathrobe, was *The Pentecostal Evangel*.

Now, in an orphanage, many boys smuggle comic books, and even off-color books, up to their rooms. Of course, when they are discovered, appropriate discipline always follows.

But these offenses are minor compared to a contraband copy of *The Pentecostal Evangel*! Even a pornographic magazine would not have caused the commotion that this magazine triggered.

Horrified, the nurse seized the magazine, ran down the corridor and the stairs, calling to the superintendent as she ran.

"Look! Look!" she cried. "Look what I found."

Rabbi Gold glanced quickly at the magazine and instantly said, "I know whose work this is. Go get Mrs. Kerr and bring her into my office right away."

Mrs. Kerr was summoned and taken to the office.

"Did you give this to Morris?" Rabbi Gold asked, sure she would deny it.

"Yes, I did," Mrs. Kerr replied simply. "I felt he should know the truth."

"The truth! The truth! Who are you to know what the truth is? Why, you're not even a rabbi!" he exploded, sure that would put Mrs. Kerr in her place.

"Well, that's true, I'm not a rabbi. But where is it written that only rabbis can know the truth about eternal things?"

Rabbi Gold did not answer. His next statement canceled any need for further discussion.

"You're fired, Mrs. Kerr," he snapped, not wanting to continue this conversation any further. "Go get your things this instant and leave this place forever. Don't say a word to anyone when you go, especially Morris."

Her heart felt as though it would break into pieces.

"O Lord, what about Morris?" she thought to herself as she left Rabbi Gold's office. "He has never really made a firm confession of You as personal Savior. He has never told me that he loves You or has accepted You."

Only two or three steps down the hall, Mrs. Kerr heard Rabbi Gold give a loud call, "Morris! Morris! Come into my office this second. I want to talk to you."

63

Morris was walking through the main corridor on his way to the kitchen. Over the office counter, Dr. Gold saw him and called to him. The young man did not know what had happened.

When Mrs. Kerr heard his name, she stopped on the stairway and began praying. "Oh, my God, what will happen to him now? Please protect him from harm."

When Morris entered the office, Rabbi Gold began, "What is the meaning of this?"

In his hand he held out *The Pentecostal Evangel.* Morris looked at the magazine, surprised to see it in the rabbi's hand.

He gulped.

He sighed.

He fidgeted.

What could he say?

Rabbi Gold did not wait for an answer.

"Morris, this is absolute trash. I don't know for sure what Mrs. Kerr has been telling you, but I do know it is all wrong. I don't ever want you to see that woman or talk to her again, is that understood?"

Morris began to cry.

In the past, when scolded by any authority, he'd respond with rebellion.

But not today.

Morris had changed.

Gone was the hard, cold, tough exterior that had been honed over years of rejection, loneliness and anger.

Something had happened.

"Listen, Rabbi Gold, I don't know much about what I've read in that magazine. I don't even understand it," Morris replied respectfully. "Even what Mrs. Kerr has been telling me is not clear. It's so different from anything I have ever heard, but I know it's real. It's real."

Then, he broke down and cried again, like he had never cried before.

"It's real!" he sobbed uncontrollably, "and you can't take it away from me!"

Mrs. Kerr smiled as she made her way up the stairs to her room to pack.

Her work had been accomplished.

Now she was satisfied in her heart.

"Oh God," she prayed to herself, "how good You are to allow me to hear this declaration by Morris before I leave this orphanage."

"I know it's real, and you can't take it from me!"

These words kept ringing in her ears.

Now she knew for certain that her job was complete, and that God would take care of Morris and complete the work He had begun in his heart. This declaration served as her reward for the great, untiring labor of love for the Master.

It was all she needed.

Her faithfulness, love and devotion had been well worth the assurance of salvation in a little wayward Jewish orphan boy's heart.

Morris now knew the reality of God and had just completed his spiritual training under Mrs. Kerr, a faithful servant in God's army.

Boot camp had ended.

Now God's chosen warrior was ready to begin his next divinely ordained step: officer's training.

SECTION TWO

MOLDED BY MIRACLES

CHAPTER SEVEN

EXODUS II

And Moses said unto God, Behold, *when* I come unto the children of Israel, and shall say unto them, The God of your fathers hath sent me unto you; and they shall say to me, What *is* his name? what shall I say unto them?

"And God said unto Moses, I AM THAT I AM: and he said, *Thus shalt thou say unto the children of Israel, I AM hath sent me unto you*"
(Exodus 3:13-14a; emphasis added).

When a solitary Hebrew named Moses confronted the mightiest king in all the world, the man of God appeared powerless.

To the officers in Pharaoh's court, Moses must have seemed a madman, coming unarmed and without any militia, to stand before the great king of Egypt and defiantly declare, "Thus saith the LORD God of Israel, Let my people go..." (Exodus 5:1b).

But Moses knew he was not alone as he stood staunchly against the Pharaoh and his vast and powerful army.

Millions of Egyptians were aghast at Moses's shocking declaration, but Moses knew he had a divine ally to help him defeat the Egyptian soldiers, who had fought major battles and conquered neighboring nations.

God was with Moses, and it was God who empowered him to lead the captive Jews out of Egypt.

To back up that seemingly ridiculous order, God gave Moses the authority to dramatically release a series of nine plagues that demonstrated who really was the ultimate authority, the ultimate power in all of Egypt.

But the Pharaoh still stubbornly resisted.

Only after every firstborn child in the land of Egypt was taken by the angel of death; only after the blood of the lamb allowed that same angel to pass over the homes of the Israelites, were the Jews finally allowed to begin their exodus from Egypt.

During their forty years of wandering in the desert, God miraculously provided His Chosen People with water from rocks, manna from the heavens, and shoes and clothing that never wore out.

God fulfilled His promise to Moses and to the Jews that He would bring them out of Egypt, free them from their bondage, redeem them, make them His people, bring them into a new land, and give that land to them for a heritage.

Four thousands years later, in 1946, another nation of Jews sought freedom from their oppressors.

But these Jews were historically and spiritually different.

They did not seem to enjoy the clear evidence of divine protection manifested for the Jews who were led out of Egypt.

When Moses and the Chosen People had to face the powerful Egyptian army, God opened up the Red Sea for them and closed it on the Egyptians, drowning the entire attacking army.

But during World War II the Jews of Germany and Europe were drowned in the Red Sea of the Holocaust.

The angel of death did not pass over six million Jewish lives.

Those remaining Jews who had voices to talk emerged from the rubble and remnants of Hitler's eradication with one solitary cry, "My God, my God, why have you forsaken us?"

In the midst of these Jewish tears, the year 1946 marked the end of Hitler's short, devastating and historically embarrassing reign of terror. The overwhelming challenge for the Jews who remained behind was to somehow begin to heal the hopelessly deep scars of genocide.

Millions of Jewish fathers, mothers, brothers and sisters had been slaughtered. Still, millions of devastated relatives remained, left with the memory of the Holocaust.

Limping, scarred, torn, raped and beaten, seemingly rejected and abandoned by their God, these unprotected Jews began to anxiously and quickly try to flee from the memories and mayhem of Europe.

In 1940, a European community of nearly 9.6 million Jews existed in peaceful harmony with their European neighbors. But through Hitler's demonic decision to systematically eradicate them in a campaign of genocide that is without parallel in all of history, their ranks were reduced to barely three million.

There were about thirty thousand survivors who were liberated from concentration camps, and another 177,000 who flew to Allied displaced persons camps following fresh persecutions in Eastern Europe.

But for most of these displaced Jews, only America or Palestine offered the slightest flicker of hope for their futures after the war.

71

The politics of Palestine was pathetic.

The British guardians of the Holy Land were bedeviled. On the one hand, they were confronted by the rising clamor of Jews demanding permission to migrate from war-torn Europe.

On the other, they were buffeted by the angry objections of the Arab states which opposed any increase in Palestine's Jewish population.

The political powers in London chose to limit the new Jewish immigration to a trickle, and the Zionist leaders of Palestine, who had all-too-recently suffered the spectacle of European Jewry's silent submission to decimation by the Nazis, wrathfully embarked on a policy of militant opposition to British policy.

An underground militia, called the Haganah, formed around a nucleus of Jewish veterans from World War II. They opened and operated an illegal immigration pipeline from Europe.

But it was not fast enough.

Slowed by the British non-cooperatives in Palestine, the Jews looked to a new promised land called America.

They came because of the Liberty Bell and Valley Forge.

They came because of the famous picture of the marines raising the flag atop Iwo Jima.

The Statue of Liberty.

The constitutional right to religious freedom.

They came because of "God Bless America," America's second national anthem during World War II. It was written by a Jew named Irving Berlin.

They knew that in America they could prove just how much the Jews would contribute if they were not burdened with the onerous taxes, pogroms, separation into ghettos, special laws and the exclusionist policies

72

Europe had heaped upon them for centuries.

For Jews, America loomed as a kind of Promised Land.

But one solitary Jew named Morris (Moses) Cerullo, in the midst of that free America of 1946, still felt captive in an unwanted land, repressed in his desire for religious freedom and dominated by an unyielding and all-powerful authority named Dr. Gold.

This one Jew vowed to escape.

But Morris knew that deep down in his heart he could count on his God as an ally and personal protector to lead him into the promised land and a new life of freedom.

CHAPTER EIGHT

WALKING
WITH ANGELS

The boy walked back to his room feeling more empty and alone than he had ever been in his fourteen plus years.

His one friend, the only adult he had grown to really know and trust, his lone spiritual teacher, Mrs. Kerr, was gone.

"Lord," he prayed, "I barely know You. I'm not even sure how to pray to You. What do I do now? Mrs. Kerr is gone. Who is going to teach me about You? Who is going to help me understand how I can better serve You? And who, dear Lord, is going to help me get rid of this aching hurt in my heart?"

His prayer was like the plaintive pleading for freedom of a captive held hostage in a foreign land.

Once, when a Jewish friend of his in the orphanage asked him about this new faith, Morris replied, "All I know is that it's real. This man named "Jesus" is real. If you ask him into your heart...He will come. So why not ask Him into your heart now, and see for yourself?"

The boy did.

"Dear Jesus, I don't understand much about You, but

75

I want to know You better. Won't You please come into my heart and help me love You? Thank You, your friend, Jimmy. Amen.''

That simple prayer of faith was honored by God, but Morris did not know how to take Jimmy to the next step, to teach that young boy about Christianity, because Morris himself did not know what to do after that confession of faith.

He could not pray "in the name of Jesus" because He was still so new in the Lord that He did not know the power that comes from praying in that name.

"I don't know," he kept answering in frustration to so many questions from those around him.

Then he would straighten his back, stand up tall, and say in his most confident young voice, "But I know it's real, and you can't take it from me. It's real, it's real, I know it's real. I cannot, I will not deny Him!"

*   *   *

This most recent incident that got young Morris into trouble was not much different from the myriad of other small infractions that invariably were blown into an explosive event by the inflammatory Dr. Gold.

"Morris, you come in here this instant and take your medicine like a man, you trouble-making little scoundrel."

Dr. Gold had run out of any patience for this rebellious youngster and really just wanted to take out his anger on the boy's body.

Here, in the basement of the orphanage, once and for all Dr. Gold had vowed he would dish out a strong enough physical punishment to make this defiant young man cease his crimes and violations against the rules of the orphanage and stop all of this nonsense about Jesus Christ being the Jewish Messiah.

A few solid, well-placed whacks and this Morris would finally behave.

As determined as Dr. Gold was to break this boy's contrary spirit, so too the fourteen-year-old victim was determined that this confrontation would be different.

With defiant eyes, Morris declared to his potential disciplinarian, "I have not fought back all this time, but if you lay your hands on me once more, I am going up to that front door and I am going to walk out forever. If I do, there's nothing you can do that can stop me, or ever get me to come back again."

Dr. Gold laughed at the youngster's declaration of freedom.

"How will you live, Master Morris? You have no clothes except the clothes on your back. You have no money. Who do you think you are...Moses? Do you think this new God of yours will provide you with manna from heaven and shoes that never wear out?"

Morris did not answer.

Instead, he turned methodically away from the taunting of Dr. Gold and started a determined walk up the stairs leading out of the basement.

He did not look to the right or the left.

Like the Jews of old, he was marching out of the bondage of his own, personal Egypt.

He was heading blindly for his promised land, trusting in a God he had never seen to be there to guide and protect him every step of the way.

He heard Dr. Gold's footsteps behind him.

At any moment, Morris expected a large angry hand to seize his small shoulder and abruptly stop his steady march towards the front door.

But there was no hand.

Morris continued to walk, step by determined step,

down the main corridor which passed by Dr. Gold's office.

Finally, he reached the front doors.

"What if they are locked?" he thought.

But when he pushed forcefully on them, they opened wide as the Red Sea, and he suddenly stood on the outside steps...free!

Freezing sleet and snow greeted Morris in the night.

"Oh great," he thought as the heavy storm pelted his bare arms and uncovered head. "What did I do to deserve this?"

For perhaps the first time in his life, this tough young child who had been forged by adversity, fired by the tossing and turnings of a cruel world, felt fear.

If this had been a movie, Morris should have flung open the doors of that orphanage to singing birds and a bright and warm sunshine on a summer day.

But this was not the movies.

The freezing night air, the sleet and snow were as real and penetrating as the lump of fear that sat solid in the pit of his stomach.

Each slap of sleet against his cheeks, each flake of snow on his forehead, seemed to shout "Go back, Morris, go back. You're not welcome here. Go back to Dr. Gold and the warm comfort of the orphanage."

But when Morris heard those two large wooden doors clang forever shut behind him at Daughters of Miriam Orphanage that night, he knew in his heart that it would be the last time he'd ever set foot inside of that orphanage again.

There was no turning back.

He began to walk, thinking to himself, "I'll head on down to Main Street where there's so much going on. Maybe I'll know what to do when I get there."

So he walked in that dark night all alone through the long solid shopping district and through one of the busiest thoroughfares in the whole state of New Jersey. A loud honk from a passing car and a "Hey kid, watch where you're going" caused him to jump up on the curb and stop to rest at a downtown street corner.

*   *   *

Mrs. Kerr was just putting on her warmest coat to go to church, when a voice inside her said, "My child, do not go to church tonight. Instead, take your umbrella and go for a walk. Let My Spirit guide you." The same God who had guided her to the Daughters of Miriam Orphanage quietly spoke to her spirit about skipping church service and walking.

In the cold night air that was becoming increasingly unpleasant, Mrs. Kerr obediently walked down one street and up another.

Finally, she ceased walking.

She knew in her heart that this was where she was to stop.

And wait.

*   *   *

The sleet and snow unceasingly pelted down on Morris's face, drenching his thin clothes, and causing goose-bumps to pop out all over his body.

His exposed face flushed red against the wind.

As miserable as he was on the outside, the inside turmoil seemed even worse.

Fourteen-and-a-half years old.

Alone.

No human being to look to for help.

In absolute desperation, he decided to pray the only kind of prayer this little Jewish orphan boy knew.

79

He lifted his eyes toward heaven and with the roller-coaster emotions rampaging within his heart, he began to sob as he spoke out loud: "Dear God, if there be such a person as Jesus up there in the heavens, please let Him be with me now."

Morris had done all he knew how to do.

He had fought against Dr. Gold and the orphanage staff until he had no emotional energy left. Although the young boy was no theological match for the well-educated rabbi, Morris never deviated from the truth as he knew it. His God was real. His Messiah was alive.

He had renounced all that was safe and secure at the Daughters of Miriam Orphanage in exchange for the cold and rainy night air.

He had left the security of hot meals, warm clothing and a clean place to sleep for the clamor of the strange and alien streets.

Now, more than ever, he needed to *know* that God was indeed paying attention to his simple little life.

Suddenly—almost instantly—after his pure prayer from the heart was over, Morris felt the mightiest of winds blow and surround him. Not a hostile, bitter wind, but the reassuring, warm, comforting, and protective presence of God.

Morris did not understand precisely what was happening, but once again there was no doubt in his mind that his Jesus was real.

"Oh, thank You, God," he sobbed. "I know You've heard my prayers. Thank You so much."

Then Morris experienced a nudging, an invisible surging on his right side, then yet another strong surging on his left side, as though there on that lonely street corner God stood as his protector on both sides!

Although Morris did not comprehend these rapid and

miraculous events, he later understood that God had sent two angels, one on his right side and one on his left, to take total charge of this fourteen-and-a-half-year-old Jewish boy and protect him.

When Morris began to further study the Bible, he would later learn he was protected...

> "Because thou hast made the LORD, *which is* my refuge, *even* the most High, thy habitation; "There shall no evil befall thee, neither shall any plague come nigh thy dwelling.
>
> "For *he shall give his angels charge over thee, to keep thee in all thy ways.*
>
> "They shall bear thee up in *their* hands, lest thou dash thy foot against a stone"
> (Psalms 91:9-12; emphasis added).

Morris felt so reassured by his divine protection that he began to sing of the heavenly joy he was experiencing. Since he knew no traditional hymns, his simple songs came straight from a child's heart, pure and holy, giving thanks to his God for the heavenly presence standing by his sides.

Now, he started to walk.

And sing.

His eyes had been closed since his simple prayer, and he started to walk. For the next two-and-one-half-miles, he walked and sang with God's presence completely surrounding him.

No words are adequate enough to express the joy, the exhilaration, the absolute happiness Morris experienced as he blindly and with a completely trusting heart allowed the two angels of God to lead him down Main Street. He traveled over curbs, across streets, through lights, past fast-moving cars all without any concern for where he was going, lost in a strange world beyond any earthly joy.

But suddenly, just as quickly as it had come, the marvelous miracle of God's guidance left. The angels were gone. He stopped singing.

"Oh God, please God, don't leave me now," Morris quickly thought.

Then he opened his eyes.

He stood directly in front of the Montauk Theater. There, under the lights, standing in the snow under an umbrella, an arm's length away from the young man, was an astounded Mrs. Kerr! She had been standing there for several hours, waiting. God had brought the two directly together that night!

"There are no words to express to God how grateful and glad I am to see you," Morris exclaimed. "I didn't know what I was going to do. Why, I don't even have money for bus fare."

They hugged and cried together.

"Morris, you come with me," a teary-eyed Mrs. Kerr told her little charge. "We'll get you out of these wet clothes as soon as possible and put you into something dry. Are you hungry?"

"Yes, yes, of course I am," is what Morris wanted to say, but his years of training in the orphanage left him restrained. His hard walls of protection from his hostile environment were still standing stiff.

"Yes ma'am, I am a bit hungry," he replied, trying hard not to shout out loud with glee for the amazing miracles God had just performed in his life.

CHAPTER NINE

LIFE FROM THE FRONT

1946 marked the beginning of a new era for the life of the fourteen-and-a-half-year-old Morris Cerullo. On the night of his orphanage exodus and his walk with the angels, Mrs. Kerr brought him to the home of Mr. and Mrs. Maurer, her brother and sister-in-law. Mrs. Kerr had brought the message of Jesus Christ to both of them, so now it seemed only fitting that they would be taking care of young Morris.

Morris had ridden on an emotional roller coaster this wonderful evening, thrust from the orphanage into the cold night, and then skyrocketed into heavenly heights as he walked with angels and miraculously met Mrs. Kerr.

But right now, even those experiences seemed to suddenly pale compared to the warmth of that fresh bowl of chicken soup that Mrs. Maurer placed before him.

"Now eat this slowly, Morris. You know your body has been through a lot tonight. No sense shocking it anymore than need be."

"Yes ma'am," Morris politely replied, fighting every urge inside of him to simply lift up the soup bowl and drink down its contents in a couple of gulps.

The rest of the evening and the conversation which took place were a blur to the tired youth.

The last thing he remembered was climbing into the bed, thinking to himself, "She must iron these sheets. I never felt anything so fresh."

*   *   *

The Sunday morning after Morris's exodus from the orphanage, Mr. Maurer asked Morris a question that would forever change the course of his life.

"Morris, you don't have to come if you don't want to, but we'd sure like to invite you to come to our church with us."

"Why of course, Mr. Maurer, I'd very much like to come with you and your family. Thank you for asking."

The Maurers attended a church in Patterson, New Jersey, called Bethany Assembly of God. It was an impressive place.

The church seated over one thousand worshipers. The entire complex was valued at more than one million dollars at the time. One stained glass window alone was estimated at thirty thousand dollars.

Bethany Assembly had started humbly in just a little storeroom. From there, it had moved to a small church building on Pearl Street, and then finally to this beautiful edifice.

When Morris entered the main auditorium with Mr. Maurer and his family, he was astounded by the long rows of pews, full of nattily dressed people.

Morris wanted to stop and sit down as soon as possible to avoid being noticed, but Mr. Maurer always had a certain place way down in front, where he was accustomed to sit for all the services. So Morris followed him nervously up the aisle.

He could not help but notice that as he passed, people

whispered to each other, some smiling broadly, others just shaking their heads as though they knew something about him that he did not know about himself.

"What is going on?" Morris thought to himself. "Why are all these people staring and looking at me? Haven't they ever seen a Jew before?"

Mr. Maurer kept walking until he got so close to the front of the church that Morris was convinced he was headed straight for the platform.

His heart was beating very fast.

It seemed like an eternity before Mr. Maurer finally reached his destination and sat down in his favorite front row pew.

Morris looked back over his shoulder, and again it seemed as though every pair of eyes were squarely focused on him.

"Welcome, brothers and sisters," Reverend David Leigh began. "The presence of God is in this place, and we rejoice in Him. Today, I ask God to bring His blessing down upon you, His people, in the name of Jesus."

And everybody said "Amen."

Then the song service began.

Pastor Leigh was an Englishman and not prone to highly emotional displays. However, in a few moments time an unusual move of the Spirit of God swept over the entire congregation. In the midst of the song service, a man in the back of the auditorium began to raise his hands and praise the Lord aloud.

When the man shouted "Hallelujah," Mr. Maurer noticed that young Morris nearly jumped three feet out of that front row pew.

Mr. Maurer was deeply concerned about how this commotion and noise would affect Morris. He silently prayed, "Lord, you know how this church likes to get blessed.

Lord, you know how we like to shout and make so much joyful noise. But today, please help keep the commotion down a bit so we won't drive away our new Jewish friend."

Morris did not understand the open display of prayerful adoration in the auditorium.

"How did I let myself get into this?" he wondered. He glanced up at Mr. Maurer and noticed beads of perspiration break out on his forehead.

After the song service, Pastor Leigh approached the pulpit to deliver his message. Although he was considered a rather reserved Bible teacher by his congregation, on this particular morning the burning coals from off the very altar of God seemed to touch his lips and set him aflame with the Holy Spirit.

Morris had never seen any rabbi conduct himself in such a manner. The young man almost became dizzy moving his head from right to left as he tried to keep his eyes focused on the preacher.

First he was here...and then he was there.

Morris thought to himself, "Why doesn't this man just stand still and preach? Why does he have to jump up and down like a kangaroo?"

Finally, the preaching ended.

It was the custom at Bethany Assembly that after the Sunday service was dismissed with prayer, the pastor would make his way to the back of the auditorium to shake hands with the people as they left the service.

Instead, on this particular Sunday morning, the people were invited down to the altar for prayer.

There was a festive mood in the air. Little did Morris realize that his own presence had triggered the outburst, for the congregation had been praying diligently for God to save his soul and bring him out of the Jewish orphanage for quite some time.

When they saw Morris walk into church on that morning with Mr. and Mrs. Maurer and Mrs. Kerr, they knew that God had indeed answered their prayers in a wonderful way.

After most of the church made their way down to the front of the altar, Mr. Maurer looked at Morris with perspiration even heavier on his face.

"Would you like to go down to the altar and pray?" he asked the young boy.

Morris looked toward the altar and then again at him. It seemed that he was almost at the altar right from where he was sitting.

"I've come this far," Morris thought to himself. "Surely a few more feet can't really hurt me."

So Morris got up and glanced around again to see if he was being watched. Then he went forward and timidly knelt at the altar.

He put his hands over his face, separating his fingers so he could see what was going on.

He bowed his head in prayer; then he lifted it up and looked around at others. He was doing more watching than praying.

An altar call was something that Morris had never seen, though he had studied for several years under the leading rabbis. He had gone to Hebrew school, became a student of the Old Testament, and knew about the experiences of the Jewish people since the time of Abraham.

They had left vivid impressions on his mind.

He knew the experiences of the Jewish people—his people—and how they had followed after God with praises upon their lips, their hands raised in holy faith before Him, and their knees bowed before the altar in expressions of humility and sincerity.

He knew that the Torah records man's dealings with God and God's dealings with man.

He knew that the spontaneous praises of God come from His people and that God even commands that His people give Him praise.

But he had never had the privilege of seeing this experience with his own eyes.

Now he saw it and felt it.

He did not consider this fanaticism or emotionalism, but people praising God and worshiping Him.

Morris knew they had something for which his heart longed. He knew that through their sincerity they had real experience with the Lord. Could he once again feel the intimacy with God he had experienced over these past few days?

It seemed to Morris as though the words of the prophet Joel were being fulfilled when he declared that in the last days, "...I will pour out my spirit upon all flesh."

Morris did not understand the move of the Spirit of God that morning, but he did not mock or laugh at it. These people had something from God and he wanted to receive that same experience.

He returned to church that Sunday night to experience the move of God in his life. That night the gifts of the Spirit of God were to be given to him.

After the preaching was finished and the altar call was given, no one had to ask him, "Would you like to go down to the altar?" Morris was the first one to step out of his seat. He rushed to the front of the altar, kneeling down near the big pulpit.

As he began to pray with lifted hands, praise to the Lord fell from his lips. Tears of humility flowed down his cheeks.

"Oh God, how grateful I am that You have saved my soul, and have given us Jesus Christ as the Messiah of the world. Oh God, how thankful I am that You have removed the scales from my eyes and allowed me to see You as a personal God. Thank You for allowing this little Jewish boy to become part of your heavenly family."

Morris had not been praying long—maybe ten minutes —when he felt as if a hand had been placed on his forehead. Something charged through his whole being. He fell prostrate to the floor.

He had never heard the terminology Pentecostals use, such as "slain by the Spirit," but there he was under the influence of the Holy Spirit. It was strange to him, since he had no knowledge or education regarding such things.

Morris felt embarrassed. He wanted to get up from the floor, but he could not move. All he could do was let the praises of God surge from his being and glorify the Lord.

Then, he began to see a beautiful vision of the sky. In a few moments, out of the sky came drops of water, large drops. Each drop of water had a word written across it in a language he did not recognize or know. As these drops came closer to him, they encompassed his whole being.

In about ten minutes, he was speaking in an unknown heavenly language. God was gloriously baptizing him with the Holy Spirit according to the promise of God:

"Then Peter said unto them, Repent, and be baptized every one of you in the name of Jesus Christ for the remission of sins, and ye shall receive the gift of the Holy Ghost. For the promise is unto you, and to your children, and to all that are afar off, *even* as many as the Lord our God shall call" (Acts 2:38-39).

This would turn out to be one of the most wonderful nights in his entire life! They stayed in the church until about one o'clock in the morning, speaking in tongues and magnifying the Lord of glory.

When they arrived home, no one could sleep. Then Mr. Maurer made a confession to Morris.

"You know, Morris, before tonight, Mrs. Kerr, my wife and I have only been dabbling in this Pentecostal thing at church. But tonight, when we saw God baptize an innocent young boy who knew nothing of His power, we now know without doubt that this powerful move of the Holy Spirit is from God."

Mr. Maurer fell to his knees. Mrs. Maurer and Mrs. Kerr dropped to their knees. The power of God moved in that house in an unusual manner. All present knew God wanted to do something more before the night was over.

In the early hours of the morning, the Spirit of the Lord came upon Morris. He stood to his feet and began to speak in tongues and interpret those unknown tongues by the Spirit into English. This continued for some time.

God had not only baptized him with the Holy Spirit, but had given the gifts of speaking in tongues and interpretation as well. Amazement filled the faces of those present as the glory of the Lord shone from his being like the sun, as he stood magnifying the Lord.

But that was not all. In a few minutes he was to experience a demonstration from heaven that surged through his whole being. He began to give forth prophecies under the anointing of the Holy Spirit.

God let it be known this evening that His divine stamp of approval was upon this life and that He had called Morris to do a special work.

CHAPTER TEN

THE FOOTSTEPS
TO HELL

And it shall come to pass in the last days, saith God, I will pour out of my Spirit upon all flesh: and your sons and your daughters shall prophesy, and *your young men shall see visions*, and your old men shall dream dreams: And on my servants and on my hand-maidens I will pour out in those days of my Spirit; and they shall prophesy" (Acts 2:17-18; emphasis added).

"What's the matter, Morris?" Mr. Maurer asked, confused about the boy's pensive mood. "You barely ate any supper tonight. You seem to be way off, as if you are floating in another world."

"Nothing," Morris mechanically replied.

He simply was not used to adults inquiring about his life and moods, so the easiest thing for him to do was to give a vague answer and hope the questioning would stop.

It didn't.

"Morris, you've been with us for several months now, and I've never seen a boy so busy, so obsessed with telling others about God. You barely took time out to celebrate your fifteenth birthday. You are a real spiritual warrior, I'll tell you that. All those Youth for Christ meetings, the youth rallies in the civic clubs and local high school auditoriums. Well, there's just been so much in your life so quick.''

Mr. Maurer paused, then asked what he was sure would be the key question. "Morris, are you feeling a bit overwhelmed by all of this?''

For the first time in this one-sided conversation, Morris reacted with a smile. He deeply appreciated what Mr. Maurer was trying to do and had to smile when he realized just how far off Mr. Maurer was from knowing what was really bothering him.

"Gosh, no, I don't feel one bit overwhelmed by all the preaching and sharing God with others. It is the thing I enjoy doing most. I wish there were time to do more. No, that's not it.''

"Then what is it?'' Mr. Maurer asked in absolute frustration, confident that something was bothering the young lad.

"O.K., O.K.,'' Morris sighed, really wanting to talk about it with somebody anyway. "I'll tell you. You see, I've always wanted to be a lawyer. Now that I am a Christian, in my heart I want to be a good Christian lawyer and serve God as the best lawyer I can be. Maybe even be governor someday.''

"Well then,'' Mr. Maurer interrupted, confident that he had the answer to this young man's problem, "then it is a Christian lawyer and the governor of the state that you shall be.''

Once again, Morris smiled.

"It's just not that simple. On one hand, as a Christian lawyer I could help people with their problems and burdens. I'd be somebody they could come to and trust to be honest. On the other hand, I feel the call of God on my life to preach. But quite honestly, that's not what

I've dreamed of doing all these years. I just don't know what to think."

"I see," Mr. Maurer replied, putting his arms around Morris. "Well, Morris, there's one thing I'm sure of... you'll do the right thing, the thing that God wants. You just keep yourself open to God's will, and He'll guide you down the right path, just like He guided you to Mrs. Kerr that rainy night six months ago."

"Yes sir," Morris replied as he watched Mr. Maurer walk into another room, confident that he'd been a big help to the boy.

$$*\qquad\qquad *\qquad\qquad *$$

An unquenchable fire burning within Morris's gut compelled him to tell others about the God who had become such a real and personal part of his life. He became almost miraculously transformed from the rebellious, Jewish orphan to a disciplined, unstoppable spiritual warrior.

He preached on the street corners and organized youth groups to sing and testify in bars. He'd book any vacant room, any civic club, any auditorium that could hold people who would come to hear his message. He preached to both denominational and non-denominational churches. Hundreds were saved by the power of God flowing through this boy in just a few months time.

Morris did not understand the first thing about homiletics or teaching the Bible. But his enthusiasm made up for his lack of experience and knowledge. He was aggressively learning on the frontlines, not out of some textbook on church evangelism.

Morris enthusiastically ministered around the entire state of New Jersey, leaving the Maurer house on the average of three to four times a week. Once, in a Baptist church in Nutley, New Jersey, at the end of his preaching, the pastor, his wife, and about thirty-five members of the congregation were wondrously born-again by the power of God.

But Morris still fought the call of God. Each time he ministered in a church or to a group, he knew the touch of God was upon his life, that God was calling him to do a work for His people. His heart was burdened as he saw the sinful condition of the world. Scarcely did he give an altar call without tears running down his cheeks. He stood there pleading and begging people to give their hearts to the Lord, Jesus Christ, and to accept Him as their Lord and Savior before it would be eternally too late.

One night, God dealt with his soul in a way that defies description. What transpired that evening would change him, the course of his life, and totally reshape his ideals, desires and ambitions.

As he was in prayer at the altar of Bethany Assembly of God in Patterson, New Jersey, he felt the hand of God come and press itself on his forehead. In the tick of a second he was overcome in the presence of God.

He did not know exactly how long he lay there, but it seemed to be quite some time before a vision began to unfold before his eyes. After the vision began, his spirit lifted from this earth and was taken right into the heavens. Morris was a chosen vessel of God, and God had ordained that he should be brought into the heavenlies and see His glory face to face like Moses did, and hear His voice like the prophets did.

Twice in his life he felt the hand of God upon his forehead. Once when he received the baptism of the Holy Spirit and again this time.

The best way I know how to describe Morris's experience is to tell you how this phenomenon appeared. It came slowly at first, one scene, then another, each piece fitting into place like a puzzle, until the complete picture was formed.

From one end of his eyes' vision to the other appeared a beautiful blue sky. It was like a maze which came before his eyes. The unusual thing about this was it did not have white running through it as you would expect to see when looking up into the sky. Just to look at it gave Morris the feeling of something supernatural.

When the vision began to appear, Morris became very nervous, at first unable to understand or comprehend what was taking place. Prostrate before the Spirit of God, his heart beat rapidly.

"Perhaps this is heaven," he thought. He had heard of the Second Coming of Christ, and that it was soon to take place. He wondered if the trumpet of God had sounded and he had been caught up to meet the Lord in the clouds. Yet, he reasoned that it could not be, for he was fully conscious and was lying here on earth prostrate before God's Spirit.

The next scene that appeared startled him. He saw, stretched from one end of that beautiful blue sky clear to the other end, millions of people from every nation of the world. They came before his eyes in rapid succession.

There was something unusual about this mass of humanity. They were not grouped together as you might expect to see a sea of people. They were seated in even, gigantic rows in a semi-circle, row upon row, as far as his eyes could see. Literally tens of millions of people.

In the midst of his wonderment, Morris was further amazed, for right in the very first row he suddenly saw himself sitting with the rest of the men and women of the world.

From the moment he saw the vision, he lost complete contact with his body on earth. It was as if he had looked into a mirror and then became part of the picture he had seen. In a single moment his spirit had somehow been snatched from his earthly body and taken into the heavenlies.

You can imagine the feeling which began to pulsate through his whole being.

He knew for sure he was in heaven, seated with that sea of people, every eye fixed straight ahead. His heart throbbed in anticipation of what would happen next.

I pause in holy awe in writing these words to you. What happened next cannot be adequately put into sentences on these pages.

Before that sea of humanity appeared a manifestation of the Godhead!

Oh, he did not see Jesus with long brown hair, a beautiful beard and a nice long white robe, but he knew it was God!

Directly in front of that magnificent mass of people, about the height of an average man, about six feet tall and two feet wide, there appeared a great flaming ball of brightness and glory.

It had no physical human features about it at all! There were no eyes, no ears, no nose, no mouth, no hands and no legs, but just a great flaming ball of brightness and glory.

When it appeared, Morris began to shake with that host of people who had also seen the same manifestation! Morris thought of how Moses must have felt when he beheld the burning bush, a bush with flames of fire, yet never consumed.

There had not been a sound made up until this time for this tremendous Presence commanded the reverence, quietness and attention of everyone.

The glory of the Presence shone as ten thousand suns

and a million moons. No words could detail its color. No vocabulary is adequate to describe its majesty.

But the Presence stood there in its crystallization of glory and brightness, causing the heavens to shine with its radiance.

The next portion of the vision which took place is even harder to describe.

Just as you might stretch forward your right hand and arm, a ray from the right side of that tremendous bright light of glory reached out in Morris's direction. The light struck his body. He felt every muscle of his whole being paralyzed by its glory. Before he knew it, Morris was standing and that light which had paralyzed his body was drawing him. He was walking towards the Presence of God. Can you imagine the sensation that struck his innermost being?

In this vision not one word was spoken, not one sound made, only the sequence of silent scenes, all combining to make this great picture.

He was walking in the heavenlies toward the manifestation of the Presence of God, for this light was the glory of the Godhead, the Father, the Son, and the Holy Spirit.

He walked toward the Presence until he got right to the place where the light was, standing perhaps an arm's length from it.

As he stood so close to God's glory, a feeling of ecstasy, a sense of complete fullness, came over him. Surely he felt that his "cup runneth over."

Then, to Morris's amazement, the Presence of God which had been so near moved about a foot away. When this happened, perplexing emotions engulfed him. He had felt so wonderful that the Presence of God had drawn him by His power right to His side, but now his heart ached as He moved a step away from him. Morris could not understand this. After the joy of being so near to God, it was terrible to feel His Presence move away.

Then his eyes were drawn downward to the place where the glory of God was standing in the heavens and, right where He had been standing, there was a hole in the sky in the form of two footprints. It was as if someone had taken a knife and cut a hole in a great big cake of cheese and one could see right through it.

When Morris looked through these footprints, what he saw and what he heard changed the course of his life, causing him to dedicate his life to winning souls and to bringing deliverance to the afflicted.

He saw through these open footprints the very flames of hell—the horrors of a literal, fiery, eternal hell. It was as though God had taken the lid off of hell. He saw the flames rising until they were burning right underneath the footprints which had been made by the Presence of God. In the midst of those flames were multitudes of lost souls, contorted in horrible anguish.

If a messenger were sent straight from hell to warn the sinner, people still would not comprehend the terror and torment that awaits the unsaved and lost in that dreadful place. Oh, the screams and the cries of those hurting souls!

Morris understood that throughout eternity torment will continually remind these souls of the awful sin of rejecting God's love when they walked on the face of the earth.

He heard the cries of sons and daughters who had rejected parental guidance and were now crying aloud for their mothers' prayers that might yet snatch them from the burning.

He heard the cries of mothers and fathers who now realized that their lives had failed to glorify God.

He heard the cries of the contrite backsliders and truly "...it had been better for them not to have known the way of righteousness than, after they have known it, to turn from the holy commandment delivered unto them" (2 Peter 2:21).

Oh, the screams for another chance, the cries and prayers that were now going up.

But there was no answer.

Truly, Morris realized that the Word of the Lord would not return unto Him void. As God has said "...I have called, and ye refused; I have stretched out my hand, and no man regarded" (Proverbs 1:24).

Morris's heart began to burn with compassion for the multitude. He knew that God, without saying a word, was asking him: "Morris, will you give Me your life totally and completely?"

Morris thought of those burning souls.

He felt in his heart insecurities similar to those Moses felt. "Lord, who am I, that I should go unto Pharaoh, and that I should bring forth the children of Israel out of Egypt?"

But, like Moses, he knew God would be with him.

And he knew what he had to do.

He put his feet into the indentations that had been made by the Presence of God, and to his utter amazement, his feet fit perfectly into those footprints...the exact size of his feet!

With a sense of deep satisfaction, Morris knew that his God had personally called him in this vision, had shown him the need, and then left the choice up to him. There was only one thing needed, and that was for him to surrender to the will of God.

By standing in those footsteps, Morris said to God, "I surrender all."

He would be the hedge for others. He would stand in the gap for lost souls.

His life would make the difference between thousands of souls falling into the pit of hell and thousands of souls walking through the gates of glory.

As he was standing in these footprints, answering the call of God, surrendering his life to God, he felt a warm sensation all around his back.

As he turned, that bright light stayed right by his side, completely surrounding him. When he put his feet into the footprints, he moved closer to the glory of God.

That ray that drew him to the Presence of God was now glowing all around his shoulders. It made him feel strong. It took away fear and nervousness, and seemed to give him an unusual power.

Until this time in the vision there had been no spoken word from this light, but now a voice spoke and said words which he did not learn until years later were based on Isaiah 60:1:

"My son, arise, shine, for thy light is come and the glory of the Lord is risen upon thee. Thou shalt not be afraid for thou shall not stand in thine own strength, neither shall you stand in thine own place but you shall stand in the place I have made for thee, and My strength shall uphold and guard thee."

As God spoke, the brilliant glory of His Presence exploded over that multitude of people, lighting up all the heavens and bathing all the people in a fabulous white light!

Then came the very last scene in this wonderful manifestation.

With a powerful force, that glorious Presence of God began to shoot rays of bright light and glory all over the heads of that sea of humanity. The last words the

Presence of God spoke to him were these:

"Son, when thou shalt see My glory in the midst of My people, know then that I am there to show myself strong in behalf of them that love **Me**, that I am there in the midst of thee to bless thee as thou shalt minister to My people."

CHAPTER ELEVEN

THE FRANCO AMERICAN YEARS

W hat's your name?'' the handsome seventeen-year-old evangelist asked the young girl sitting next to him.

"Theresa LePari," she replied, paying little attention to the inquiry of the man sitting next to her. "Would you please pass the butter?"

"Sure," the young man replied, reaching for the butter dish without ever taking his eyes from her.

He was secretly thankful that Reverend Nickolof, the president of Metropolitan Bible Institute, had asked him to minister his testimony at the chapel service today. Looking at Theresa's lovely face made him feel very happy indeed that he had accepted the invitation.

"She's about the most exciting thing that's happened to me since I've come to Suffern, New York," he thought to himself.

"You know, Theresa, there's something I want to share with you," the young man said as they ate their lunch. He had hoped his statement would get her attention away from the dinner salad she was eating.

He noticed that every bite she took was methodical

and planned. If one piece of lettuce had a brown spot on it, or looked wilted, she pushed it aside in favor of a nice fresh piece. As he watched her pick through her salad, he could not believe what he was about to say. He heard the words in his mind, felt them deep in his soul, and *knew* that they would come true. Yet, somehow, he could not understand why or how he could possibly be sharing them with her now without sounding too foolish.

"I have a call on my life from God," Morris began in a very serious tone. "After I finish my studies, I'm going to preach the gospel and reach souls for Jesus Christ."

"That's why we are all here," Theresa replied, as though Morris were only stating the obvious. "All of us want to serve God just like you do."

"Oh, I know that all the Bible students want to serve God," Morris answered, sure she did not grasp the depth and significance of what he was trying to convey to her. "But the Bible says 'Many are called, but few are chosen.' I don't mean this to sound like I am something special, Theresa, but in my heart I know that God has chosen me to reach thousands of lost souls."

He stopped suddenly, feeling that perhaps he had already said too much. "I don't even know why I am telling you this. I just wanted you to know."

Theresa heard, but did not react.

After the luncheon, the two were walking together across the field towards the women's dorm where Theresa stayed.

Just as they were about to part, Morris once again felt strongly impressed to say something significant that came from deep within his spirit to this young and very attractive lady.

"Theresa LePari," he began, stopping his walk so he

could look her straight in the eyes, "there's something else you should know about me."

"What's that?" she asked, sure that this man she had already decided was arrogant and rather boastful was going to say something further about his "chosen" calling for lost souls.

"You may not believe this now, but you should know that someday I'm going to marry you."

Upon hearing that declaration of intent, the dark-haired beauty screamed at the top of her lungs and ran full speed towards her dormitory! As she got to the safety of her room, she slammed shut the door and locked it.

She thought to herself, "Why, that boy is crazier than I thought! Who does he think he is telling me I'm going to marry him? I don't even know him. What a strange one that fellow is," she thought, her heart still pounding from the long run.

"Besides," she added as if to convince herself that this marriage would be impossible, "I'm already engaged, and I'm sure my fiance would have something to say about my getting married to Morris."

Morris walked off the campus of the Metropolitan Bible Institute that day with a little smile on his face, knowing full well he would return at another time to fulfill his spontaneous declaration to marry Theresa.

He knew it from the first time he saw her.

Someday, some way, she'd be his wife.

As he unlocked the door to his car, Morris still had that slight smile on his face. The memory of Theresa running toward her dorm burned deep in his mind.

He did not see Theresa again until that summer.

*   *   *

"Hello, Theresa, this is Morris...Morris Cerullo. Listen, I just happened to be in the city today, so I thought I'd give you a call and come to see you."

There was an air of confident assurance in the young man's voice.

"Oh, I'm sorry, Morris, I just don't think...."

"Who is it, dear?"

"Someone from school, Mother."

"Who?"

"That Morris Cerullo."

"Well, don't keep him hanging on the phone, invite him over for supper."

"I heard that," Morris announced on the other end of the phone. "Your mom is so nice. Tell her I accept her invitation and I'll be right over. Bye."

Before Theresa could lodge her protest, the loud buzzing of a dead phone rang in her ear. In what seemed like only a few minutes, there was a knock on the door. Mrs. LePari opened it.

"Why hello, Morris, come on in," Mrs. LePari said. She had met young Morris at the Metropolitan Bible Institute and liked him very much. After all, they had a sort of kinship since they had both been raised in orphanages.

"These are for you, Mrs. LePari," Morris said as he walked through the door, handing her a box of candy. "Mostly all chocolates."

"Why thank you, Morris, they're my favorite kind. Theresa's in the kitchen."

"And the food smells really good, too."

Morris was always the diplomat and knew how to win over Theresa's mom, even if he had not yet won over Theresa's heart. "Let's see, this is Sunday, so it must be spaghetti."

"That's right, Morris," Mrs. LePari laughed. "Just what any self-respecting Italian family cooks on a Sunday afternoon."

106

"Oh Lord, he's here," Theresa thought to herself as she heard the voice in the other room. "Why doesn't he just go away and leave me alone?"

She quickly took off her soiled apron and put on a nicely ironed one as she straightened up her hair a bit. "Doesn't he know I am not interested in him?" she thought, checking the mirror quickly to make sure she looked presentable. The mirror reflected one of the prettiest young ladies in all the county.

"Hello, Theresa," Morris said as he entered the kitchen. "Your mom told me I'd find you here. She sure is a nice lady. I really like her."

"Hi, Morris," Theresa replied, feigning disinterest. "Hope you didn't come much out of your way to visit us."

"Oh no, no trouble at all. Was just in the neighborhood so thought I'd stop by and see how your summer's going."

"Fine, thank you," she replied, stirring the simmering sauce, trying to be as nonchalant as possible.

"Theresa, why do you try so hard to pretend you don't like me?" Morris asked, never one to avoid tricky subjects with anyone.

Theresa gave the straightforward question an equally straightforward answer.

"Because you are so arrogant," she said without even thinking. "You act like you know exactly what you want out of life and how you are going to get it. That makes me mad."

Morris was very serious now.

"Is it arrogance if I *do* know where I am going and I *do* know what I want to do? I know without a shadow of doubt that God has called and chosen me to be a preacher, and so that's what I'm going to be. How does that make me arrogant?"

107

"Oh Morris," Theresa replied, putting the spaghetti into the boiling water and stirring it slowly, "I don't know, you just seem to come across that way. Maybe you can't help it, I don't know."

*   *   *

After dinner, Theresa and Morris went for a walk and talked.

"How many are in your family, Theresa?" Morris asked.

"I have two brothers and three...well, two sisters now. Marie died when I was just thirteen years old. She was the oldest."

"That death must have been quite a shock."

"Marie's death changed my life," Theresa replied with a tear in her eye. "Most of our years growing up we were not very close. She was four years older, and Mom and Dad favored her. When the dishes needed to be done, I always had to do them, not Marie. When the kitchen floor had to be scrubbed, I had to do it, not Marie. That kind of built up some resentment in me, you know what I mean?"

"Yes, I can imagine it would," Morris replied, thinking of all the hundreds of times in the orphanage when he had to do the work while the older boys watched. "So what changed your attitude?"

"Well, this may sound cruel, but while Marie was very sick, hardly able to move, and unable to walk anymore, I had to do the family wash in our old wash tub. I was murmuring and complaining about it. Probably too loud, 'cause Marie heard me. When I faced her in her room, she looked me in the eyes and said, 'Theresa, I wish I could trade places with you.' "

Morris took Theresa's hand into his own and gave it a tender squeeze, as he noticed Theresa's eyes moist with tears. She paused a second to regain her composure, then continued.

"Oh Morris, when she said that to me, how could I resent her anymore? I forgave her and hugged her and kissed her and told her I was sorry for being so selfish. Of course, at thirteen I suppose I was the typical self-centered teenager, but Marie opened my eyes to some very deep feelings. After that conversation with Marie, I always did my wash and other chores, including cooking the spaghetti on Sunday, with a smile on my lips."

"That's a beautiful story, Theresa, thanks for sharing it with me," Morris said as he took her back to the door. "Do you mind if I take you out to dinner sometime soon...say, next week?"

"Yes, yes, that would be fine," Theresa replied without thinking, surprised at her own answer.

"I'll call you Tuesday and set up a time," Morris said as he opened the door to her house.

"O.K. That'll be fine. Goodnight."

*   *   *

Reverend Nickolof was looking at one of the prettiest brides to ever walk down the aisle of this humble church in Newburg, New York. As president of the Bible College, he knew and loved both of these kids getting married this day. The ceremony had a special meaning to him, like marrying part of his family.

"Don't know how Morris pulled this off," he thought to himself. "Theresa being engaged to marry Danny and all. Who knows, or can begin to understand, the wonders of young romance?"

The organ music jolted him back to attention.

The beautiful bride walking down the aisle had all eyes focused on her. And no wonder! She radiated that special beauty reserved only for a young girl's wedding day.

109

As she walked...no, floated down the aisle...in her homemade white satin gown, quiet gasps of admiration could be heard coming from the congregation.

There were layers of lace flowing down the front of her dress, carefully appointed with little satin covered buttons. Theresa had lovingly stitched every section of her "sweetheart" neckline, and her long, pointed, puffy sleeves were plain, yet elegant. A long train glided behind her, and on her head she wore a little beaded cap she had crafted herself.

Morris stood waiting at the end of the aisle in a simple white jacket that could not hide his muscular build that came from his participation in high school baseball, football and basketball.

As Mrs. LePari stared teary-eyed at her daughter, then at the handsome young Morris, she quietly chuckled to herself as she remembered that time in the kitchen with Theresa and Danny.

"Now Theresa, you are going to have to tell the truth about this. Right now I want you to make up your mind about this thing. Danny, sit down at the table and drink some coffee and have a danish."

"Yes, ma'am," he replied, not having the slightest idea what "this" was about.

"Now Theresa, this thing is getting serious. It is either one or the other. You have got to know who you really love. This is for the rest of your life. So Theresa, what is your answer to Danny?"

Theresa was furious at her mother for putting her in such a difficult spot. Yet somehow she was grateful that the problem would finally be over.

In her bravest voice, she spoke these words as tenderly and as gently as she knew how to her fiance: "Danny, I'm sorry, but I've got to break off our engagement. I'm afraid I just can't marry you. I'm so very sorry...."

"I can't believe what you are saying," Danny said in total shock. "Theresa, let's discuss this, O.K.? Surely you don't mean what you are saying."

"I'm afraid there's nothing to discuss, Danny," Theresa said. "I know this is very sudden, but I have made up my mind."

"I just can't believe this," Danny repeated again, unable to bear any more of this one-sided, devastating conversation.

Jumping up to leave, he spilt his coffee. He ran out the backdoor and right to the same church where they were all gathered today, crying his eyes out.

"Dearly beloved..." the preacher began, snapping Mrs. LePari back to attention.

Mr. LePari sat very proud as he watched the lovely couple say their wedding vows.

"Morris is a hard worker, a fine man," he thought to himself, remembering how he often worked two or three jobs to get himself through Bible college. "He's painted, fixed roofs, washed dishes, cooked—anything to make a few dollars. He'll take good care of my little girl."

$$* \qquad * \qquad *$$

"Morris, do you really think we should go to a ball game? You know how strict our church is about these things. Some even consider it a sin."

"Now Theresa, God knows our hearts. He knows we are on our honeymoon and are entitled to a little fun and relaxation. Honey, it's 1951, not the time of Jesus. Anyway, I'm sure if they had baseball games in His day, He would have gone to one once in a while. God doesn't mind, and He's the only One important whose opinion matters to me."

So they went.

That night, after the game, Morris parked his father-in-law's car up on the hill near the place where they were staying with some friends. The bright shiny Chevy either had poor brakes or Morris did not secure them tightly enough. Whatever the cause, the car rolled down the hill and smashed to a halt!

Every bit of the young couple's honeymoon money went into repairing that car perfectly before returning it to the unsuspecting father-in-law.

Those who supposedly knew about these spiritual things said the car rolled down that hill because "God was punishing those youngsters because they didn't do right. That's what they get for wasting their time by going to that baseball game."

*   *   *

"Don't forget these," Theresa said, handing her new husband the sheets and towels they had received as wedding gifts. "Hope there's room for everything. It would hardly be fitting for a new pastor's wife not to have clean towels."

The car was stuffed with new items from two wedding showers, plus an old sewing machine Theresa's grandmother had given her. "Well, it's off to Claremont, New Hampshire," Morris said, letting Theresa know it was time to get into the car. Deep inside, he was anxious to report to his first pastorate. The drive there was uneventful.

When they arrived at their new apartment, the newlyweds immediately faced some of those classic, once-in-a-lifetime struggles that seem to be so vital in molding young marriages into successful long-term relationships. They had no furniture, no table or chairs, and no bed to sleep in.

They simply stood in an empty, rented apartment with almost no worldly possessions.

"Are you hungry?" Morris asked his young bride after their trip.

"Sure am," Theresa replied, knowing full well there wasn't much to eat. "What tasty morsel should we devour first?"

They both laughed, knowing they had just exhausted all of their start-up living funds in repairing that smashed car.

"I've got just the ticket," Morris said, reaching into a grocery bag. "Madam, if you please, allow me," Morris suggested, graciously motioning for Theresa to sit down on the kitchen floor.

In his most expressive manner, Morris picked up the can opener and with all the flair of a high-priced waiter at an elegant restaurant opened a can of Franco American spaghetti as their first meal together in their first home.

Since they did not have a pot to cook it in, Morris carefully warmed the bottom of the can on the stove, careful to take the top portion for himself so Theresa would get the hot spaghetti closer to the bottom of the can.

Morris was smiling to himself.

"What is it, honey?" Theresa asked.

"Oh, I was just thinking. Here we are, sitting on this cold hardwood floor, eating a can of spaghetti, with maybe two nickels between us...and you know what... I've never been happier in my life!"

Putting down her bowl of spaghetti, Theresa gave Morris a loving hug that said "I know, I know."

Morris's love for Theresa grew even deeper as he watched her eat the simple meal.

He knew Theresa was always very selective about the food she ate...had been from the first day he saw her at that Bible college luncheon...yet here she was, on a cold floor, eating canned spaghetti without a complaint.

He felt warm inside, knowing she must love him very much.

When it came time for bed, they moved from the kitchen floor to the bedroom floor.

In their wedding showers, they had been given sheets, blankets, and pillows...but no bed.

So they slept on the floor.

Later, a friend would provide them with a used mattress, but the young couple did not buy anything new until they had saved all the money.

Then they bought a couch, a couple of chairs and a bedroom set.

It took months to save for these items, because even as a young man, Morris always refused to buy anything on credit.

SECTION THREE

SEASONED FOR SERVICE

CHAPTER TWELVE

EXPLODING BREAKTHROUGHS IN A SHRINKING UNIVERSE

T he narrow focus of nations inward towards isolationism began to change drastically as the 1950's dawned on the world scene. What radically shifted the focus from "me" to "they" really started in 1946 with the first call to order of the United Nations General Assembly in London. This international assemblage marked an unprecedented attempt for "world neighbors" to communicate and exist with each other on a diplomatic rather than a military basis, to anticipate and avoid trouble before it escalated into violent conflict.

The U.N. challenged nations to place their actions under the scrutiny and judgment of others whose locations were often thousands of miles away. The world had shrunk. The ravages of World War II, combined with the all-too-sudden outburst of the Korean War from 1950 to 1953, clearly announced that the era of isolated nations going about their own destiny without regard to how their actions affected the territory of other countries was doomed.

An era of cooperation between western nations emerged with the establishment of NATO (the North

Atlantic Treaty Organization) in 1949. Twelve nations agreed to work together for mutual defense.

But the elusive desire for peace was not the only bond bringing nations together. For the sake of profit and prosperity, in 1951 six nations decided to pool European coal and steel resources. The European Economic Community, more commonly known as the European Common Market, was founded in 1958, thus admitting that the financial future of one nation was somehow tied to the financial future of neighboring nations.

And the world shrunk a little more.

In the early fifties, television was introduced in the United States. That invention forever changed the possibility of a nation, or even a single family, remaining isolated from the world.

Even a rural family living in the most remote area through the miracle of the little electronic box could watch global events unfold in the privacy of their own living room. It was as though they were standing on the sidewalk when a king was crowned or sitting in the back seat of a convertible in Dallas when a president was shot.

The constant cry of the fifties centered around peaceful co-existence. Every nation knew that the escalation of the weapons of warfare had made the very survival of the earth an issue for the first time in human history. War no longer just damaged the participants in the conflict, but had the potential to destroy the entire planet as well!

When one nation fought against another, all were somehow affected in this shrinking world.

Peace became the cry of the decade.

Global cooperation became the visible means to peace.

Military might became the way to enforce that peace.

President Truman gave the orders for the development of a hydrogen bomb. Within six years of his challenge, on May 21, 1956, the first aerial H-bomb was tested over Namu Islet, Bikini Atoll. The blast equaled a total of ten million tons of TNT.

Never before in the history of the world had there ever been such a mighty explosion!

In 1957, the vision of the world as "neighbors" expanded even further—towards the heavens—when the Russians launched "Sputnik I," the first earth-orbiting satellite, marking the beginning of what became known as the Space Age. And the world shrunk a little more. Spy satellites were developed to pry into the privacy of a nation's backyard.

In 1960, the top Nazi murderer of Jews, Adolf Eichmann, was captured by Israelis in Argentina and executed in Israel in 1962.

A German.

Caught by Israelis.

While living in Argentina.

The world indeed was shrinking.

When John F. Kennedy was inaugurated as president of the United States in 1961, he immediately challenged America to care about the welfare of other nations by introducing the Alliance for Progress, a ten-year plan to raise Latin American living standards.

Then, he challenged America to expand their vision beyond the earth, beyond even merely orbiting the globe, by declaring that America would send a man to the moon.

That explosive concept of space exploration was paralleled in the U.S.S.R. by an explosion of a different sort.

In 1961, Russia fired a fifty-megaton hydrogen bomb... the biggest bomb blast in history. The force of this bomb was five times more powerful than the one exploded just five years before by the U.S.

It was in this historically unprecedented climate of nation interacting with nation, in this explosive world of hydrogen bombs, in this visionary world of space exploration that Morris Cerullo lived as he journeyed to his first international crusade in 1955.

CHAPTER THIRTEEN

"DADDY, WHAT STATE IS ATHENS IN?"

Honey, what does it say?'' Theresa asked, discreetly straining to read over his shoulder to read the airmail letter with the foreign-looking stamp.

"It's an invitation to come to Athens, Greece, to hold crusades," Morris replied seriously, folding up the letter quickly. "Reverend Koustis, the superintendent of the Church of God in Greece, wants me to come right away."

"Why, honey, that's great! You were so right when you told me two weeks ago that God was preparing your heart to go to Athens, Greece," Theresa said, hugging her husband.

A feeling of deep pride warmed her heart.

"You always knew in your spirit that someday God would take you to the foreign fields to fulfill the vision He gave to you. And now, it's coming to pass!"

But twenty-four-year-old Morris was in a pensive mood.

He felt both excited at the possibility of going to a foreign nation for the first time, of being used by God to reach beyond America, and yet, he felt burdened by

121

the thought of being separated from his precious wife and two children.

For the last four years, he had taken his wife everywhere with him.

And when David and Susan were born, the four of them all crammed together in their car with clothes, diapers and other necessary traveling supplies and drove from meeting to meeting across the United States.

It was tough and exhausting. But at least they were together as a family.

For a moment, Morris remembered his orphanage years. Rabbi Gold had taught such strong Jewish traditions and family values. Those traditions and family values had become an important and vital part of Morris's life.

"If I decide to accept this invitation to go to Greece," he thought, "the hardest part will be having to be away from Theresa and my children even for a few weeks. I swore in that orphanage that my children would never be lonely and suffer the pains of being without a mother or father. Yet, now that God is opening to me this opportunity to minister in a foreign land...."

He paused, not completing the thought. He already knew in his spirit what he must do. But being obedient to God's will, and being God's faithful servant, never exempts a man from the pangs of separation he feels as a husband and a father.

The year was 1955. God had already blessed Theresa and Morris with two children; David was three, and little Susan was just barely one year old.

The four Cerullos traveled together in their car, Mama doing the washing and diapers wherever she could, Papa helping out, trying to make each town's hotel room feel somehow a little bit like a "home."

Morris and Theresa tried very hard to do the things normal families do, no matter what city they were in.

On Saturdays or Sunday afternoons after church, they would always go play in the park with their kids or take long walks and talk.

But after years on the road, the Cerullo family car had become a little too small to be called "home," especially after the arrival of David and Susan. So, Morris and Theresa were just completing the process of getting ready to buy their own dream home in Newburgh, New York, when that letter arrived.

Their "dream home" was a cute little three-bedroom, brick house, split level, selling for $13,500. The kitchen had white walls with a black counter top, and a black and white tile floor. It had a living room and dining room with beige carpets, and one bathroom. Yes, it was a bit small, but to Theresa and Morris, it seemed perfect.

The traveling Cerullo family had skimped and saved for years from the precious offerings Morris received on the road. And now, finally, they had saved enough money up to put a small down payment of $600 on their first home. It was all set. But when that letter came with the foreign stamp, that invitation to go to a foreign land, that challenge by God to expand the ministry beyond America, the final closing process had to be put on hold until Morris returned from his ministry to Greece.

*   *   *

"Daddy, what state is Athens in?" little David asked on the way to the airport.

"It's not in the United States, honey," his father replied, giving David a gentle rub on his head. "It is in a country across the ocean called Greece."

"Is that why you are taking a plane, Daddy?" David asked.

"That's right, David, the only way to get to Greece from New York is by an airplane. Daddy was blessed by a lady who God miraculously healed in one of his services. She was led by God to give Daddy the trip money—the exact $865.50 I needed for the plane ticket to fly there."

"Is that more than twenty-five cents?" David asked, wanting to know how that amount compared to the money he had saved in his own piggy-bank.

"Yes, son, it's a bit more than twenty-five cents."

When the family arrived at the airport, it was a scene none of the four Cerullos were familiar with. They had never been separated. Mama Cerullo tried to be brave, especially for David's sake, but already there were tears in her eyes and in David's as well.

They passed with Daddy through the airport checkout, and watched helplessly as he entered the long gateway that would take him to his four-motor airplane and to his long flight to Greece. After Morris hugged and kissed the entire family, he walked straight towards the plane, not looking back.

Theresa understood. She saw the steel-eyed, flint look on his face and knew that already his mind was purposed to his new, God-given objective: to penetrate the island of Greece with the gospel of Jesus Christ. It was like sending a general off to the front lines.

As the plane took off, Morris immediately began to pray for the people of Athens. He spent the next several hours in deep prayer, asking God for protection and binding the forces of evil.

On the way home, David was silent. Theresa spoke first.

"Even though we are not going with your daddy on this trip," she began softly, "I want you to know we are still with him, just like we have been all these times in the states. God knows we are giving Daddy up to minister in Greece, so whatever rewards Daddy receives in heaven, you and I and Susan will share in them, too. We sent our daddy off today so others very far away could know about the love of Jesus."

David just smiled, and put his arm around his mother. Sometimes the world of a three-year-old is very complicated.

When they got home, Theresa tucked David into bed and put Susan into her crib. Before they went to sleep, she started to read to them out of the Bible. Of course, baby Susan could not understand the words, but the tone of her mother's love and warmth soothed the little baby into a gentle sleep.

"And he took a child, and set him in the midst of them: and when he had taken him in his arms, he said unto them, 'Whosoever shall receive one of such children in my name, receiveth me: and whosoever shall receive me, receiveth not me, but him that sent me' " (Mark 9:36-37).

*   *   *

The plane landed in Athens and Morris Cerullo was warmly greeted by his hosts. Then, as if Satan wanted to serve notice on him immediately that this would be a time of intense spiritual warfare, Morris was greeted with incredible news.

"We could not advertise your meetings," he was told as they gathered the luggage and headed towards the hotel room.

"You see, in Greece, before we can have an evangelistic meeting, we must first secure a permit. But the only church that is allowed permits is the Greek Orthodox Church. So, as of today, we have been unable to secure that government permit. So we are not allowed to even advertise the meetings. Getting the permits has proven to be impossible."

Morris smiled slightly. He immediately recognized what was going on.

"Let me tell you something," he began in a confident, assured tone, "nothing is ever easy or routine when you are waging spiritual battle with the enemy. He fights and kicks and scratches to keep every bit of his vile territory. The fact that we do not yet have a permit for the meeting only means that God intends to unleash some mighty miracle breakthroughs in your country before we are through."

His hosts were very excited.

"Then you will come with us tomorrow morning and help fight for the necessary permits with the government authorities?" they asked.

"No, not at all," Morris replied. "We are not in a war with the government authorities. Take me to my hotel room. I will stay there and pray, and God will make a way."

The host took Morris to a little dark, dingy room in the city where arrangements had been made for him to stay. It was at the top of several flights of stairs. It had only one chair and a bed. There were no sheets, no pillow cases, just an old smelly, dirty mattress.

Morris Cerullo thought to himself, "This room almost seems symbolic of the tremendous spiritual stagnation in this nation."

That night was a night to remember. He was in a strange country, didn't know a soul, had no one to talk to and no meetings to preach in.

Morris stayed up all night praying.

*   *   *

Early the next morning, Morris left that awful room. With the little money he had saved for this missionary journey, he walked the unfamiliar streets of Athens with his two suitcases in his hands to find a better place to stay.

Finally, he located a room in a little hotel on Constitution Square and contacted his host to tell him the new room location should anything develop concerning the evangelistic meeting.

Then Morris locked the door and fell on his face before God.

"Oh, Lord, what am I going to do?" Morris cried.

No one could help him. He needed a supernatural intervention in these circumstances. He needed a miracle.

"How long has he been locked up in there?" one of the hotel employees asked.

"Two, three, four days...I don't know. Every time I go past his door, I hear him praying. Sometimes shouting, 'In the name of Jesus, devil, be bound. You have no hold on this nation. You have no right to this city. I command you to let go, in the name of Jesus.' "

The weapons of the world's warfare are readily apparent.

M-16 rifles.

Hand grenades.

Nuclear and hydrogen bombs.

But in that small hotel room in Athens, Greece, another type of warfare was being waged.

This spiritual war would have a significant impact on the nation of Greece, and begin to change the course of spiritual history in that nation.

Spiritual warfare...this was Morris Cerullo's God-given weapon, and he was using it to its fullest as he prayed and began to take this first of 130 nations for the glory of God.

God heard this humble Jew's prayers.
And He began to move.

*   *   *

One day quite unexpectedly there was a knock on his door. Morris opened the door and there stood a well-dressed lady in the hallway.

"Brother Cerullo, my name is Mrs. Torakes. I'm the wife of the vice-president of the Bank of Athens. May I come in?"

"Yes," he answered, wondering why God had brought this distinguished lady to his door. "Come in. How can I help you?"

"Brother Cerullo, I am going to share with you a strange story. It happened only recently, about two weeks ago, and it has changed the course of my life.

"I was walking down the street when I heard music coming from a room on the second floor in one of the buildings. I ventured up the stairway into a small room where a little group of Foursquare people had assembled for a midweek service. There in that group of strangers I surrendered my heart to the Lord Jesus Christ."

She paused, wiping a tear from her eye.

"Praise God," Morris replied, "then you are a born-again Christian."

"Thank you," Mrs. Torakes replied, regaining her composure and continuing her story.

"During the days that followed, I learned that you were coming from America to hold miracle services. And now, I've been told about your problems getting a permit to conduct the meetings. I want you to know that I am going to ask my husband to use all of his influence to make it possible for you to conduct your meeting."

"Well, I can certainly use all the help I can get in this

128

matter," Morris replied. "Thank you very much for your kindness."

After a bit more discussion, Morris showed the lady out the door, and got back on his knees in prayer for the next two days.

*   *   *

There was a hurried, loud knocking on his door.

"I'm coming. I'm coming," Morris Cerullo yelled.

But the knocking continued in a rapid fashion until he opened the door.

"Brother Cerullo, you won't believe it," his host said, bursting into the room, not even pausing to say hello. "It is a miracle. It is a miracle. The premier himself, George Papadopoulos, has heard our petitions and has granted the necessary permits!

"Brother Cerullo, you don't know what this means. He heard that a man of God was in the country to pray for the sick and help the lame walk, and he ordered a permit to be drawn up. This is unheard of! That a permit for an evangelistic meeting would ever be granted in this country.

"The permit was obtained through the influence of that powerful lady whose husband is the vice-president of the Bank of Athens...."

"No, no, no," Morris Cerullo interrupted. "It was not because of a powerful woman's husband that we obtained our permit. It was because we serve a powerful God. Give God the glory for this miracle. Our strength is never in man. Our strength is in our God and our works are the works of the Holy Spirit. God heard our prayers, and He wants many people to know the message of His love and salvation.

"Praise God. Let's say a prayer of thanks now to our God, and then, let's roll up our sleeves and get started on the details for our meetings.''

*　　　　　*　　　　　*

The posters were unique in the modern history of Greece.

They invited people to come to the Kentragon Theatre in Athens for an evangelistic meeting and an evening of miracles. ''The blind will see, the lame will walk, the deaf will hear,'' they proclaimed, inviting all to come.

Never before had a permit been granted for anything but the Greek Orthodox church! Yet, the crusade group was allowed to rent a building, print and distribute hand-bills, and buy ads in newspapers inviting people to come.

And they came.

The night of the meeting, there was still one major problem left to solve: Morris Cerullo needed an inter-preter, since he did not speak Greek. The only person fluent enough in Greek and English to help was a mis-sionary woman, and the pastors were concerned that a woman interpreter would not be well accepted by the conservative public.

As Morris was preparing for the meeting that night, he received a telephone call in his hotel room at 6 p.m., one hour before the meeting was to begin.

The man on the other end of the line asked, ''Is this Morris Cerullo?''

''Yes, who is this?'' Morris replied.

''You don't know me, but I am your interpreter,'' came the reply.

Morris was taken by surprise.

''Who are you?''

''I am Reverend Frangus, general superintendent of all the Assemblies of God in Greece,'' he answered. ''No one expected me; I'm just here by accident. I happened to be on a field missionary trip.

130

"I called our missionary in Athens. She told me that you were conducting services and that you needed an interpreter. I just want you to know I am rushing to your hotel right now. So just hold on. I'll be there right away."

Morris hung up the phone and thanked God for His loving grace. Morris now understood better than ever before that he was not in Greece by accident. God indeed had arranged it all. That night, when he opened his meeting, Morris Cerullo discovered that God had given him the best interpreter an evangelist could ever have.

Morris Cerullo began his first meeting with the words, "I come to you tonight in the name that is above all names, the name of Jesus Christ."

At atmosphere burst upon that auditorium like that compared to the early days of the apostles when Paul, another Jew, started preaching at Philippi in the northeast corner of Greece and established the first European Church.

So great was the anticipation that the sick were carried to the entrance of the auditorium. They fervently believed that if they could just touch Morris as he walked past, they would be healed.

Revival broke out at the Kentragon Theatre in Athens, Greece. Healings and salvations happened all over the auditorium. Hundreds were saved.

The love of Jesus was shown to many people who had been in the dark. So powerful were the meetings that they met night after night. Until one night, at the scheduled end of the crusades, the local pastors and crusade organizers came to Morris Cerullo in tears.

"Brother Cerullo, we've never seen anything like this in our country. Please do not stop the meetings. Please stay and continue them longer."

"I would love to continue the meetings," Morris

replied, "but I am out of money. I'm flat broke. And we are not allowed to take offerings in the meetings, so there's nothing else I can do. God will have to provide the way."

Then Morris thought to himself, "God, how can I tell these precious people no? Your spirit and anointing is increasing in the meetings by the day. Lord, show me a way to stay."

That night, in the privacy of his hotel room, Morris again prayed for the deepest desires of his heart.

"Lord, You hear what these ministers are asking me. They have told me of the stripes on their backs that they have received for the sake of the Gospel. Now the freedom is here. Lord, they don't want this meeting to close. I don't want it to close, but I don't know what to do."

In the still of that room, God spoke to Morris words that shocked him: "Son, you've got the money."

"Oh great! This is wonderful," Morris said. "I've got the money! Lord, do You mind telling me where I've got the money? If You tell me where it is, I'll go get it."

God answered by saying, "You've got it at home."

Morris shuddered inside.

He thought of Theresa and the kids.

He thought to himself, "Lord, you wouldn't ask that! Surely You are not asking me to give the money that Theresa and I have in the bank for our little dream house. Lord, I can't do that. I can do a lot of things but I can't do that. That has to be Theresa's decision."

*   *   *

"Can you hear me all right, honey?" Morris screamed into his phone.

Theresa was so glad to hear her precious husband's voice; she knew the reason he had not called before was because it was so expensive.

And in her spirit, she knew why he was calling now.

"Are you and the kids okay?" Morris asked, confident of her answer.

"Yes, yes, yes...we're all fine...we just miss you. How are the meetings going?" Theresa asked, wanting to make it a bit easier for her husband to ask.

"Terrific. Terrific. The power of God is so strong. Every night we are seeing hundreds of salvations and mighty miracles are manifesting themselves in so many areas."

Then there was a long pause.

"Honey, they want me to stay for more meetings. The ministers here are crying, begging me to stay longer. But I can't go on with the meeting. I don't have any more money."

"I know, Morris, I know," Theresa replied. "Sweetheart, I know why you're calling. You want me to take the money for our new house and send it to you."

Morris knew this was a sensitive and delicate moment. He resented the fact that they had to shout over the phone to be heard at such a tender time.

"Theresa," Morris shouted, "I didn't ask you to do that. I won't ask you for that money."

"Oh, you don't have to ask. That money is not my money or your money. It is God's money. If He wants us to give it for the revival to continue, then we will give it. There will always be other houses, but this is God's timing for many people in Athens. I'll send it out to you right away."

"Theresa, I love you so much," Morris shouted through the buzzing line, as he wiped away a tear from his eye.

"I love you, too, honey," she replied, not sure he heard her tender reply.

133

In the spirit, over those thousands of miles, it was as though they were standing in the same room embracing in one of the most intimate hugs in the history of their marriage. Somehow, they never felt closer.

The next day, Theresa withdrew all of their savings from the bank and wired it to her husband. It was enough to continue the meetings.

*   *   *

"Here he comes! Here he comes! Here he comes!" shouted David at the top of his three-year-old lungs. "Daddy's home! Daddy's home!" he shouted, and immediately broke through a crowd of people at New York International and rushed into his father's open arms.

Tears poured out of Theresa's eyes.

Tears poured from Morris's eyes.

"Honey, this is it," Morris said, reaching into his pocket to pull out a few coins. "This is all that's left...."

"It doesn't matter," Theresa replied, hugging her husband again. "We are together again, that's all that matters. God will take care of the rest."

In these past few weeks, God had made the nation of Greece a place of spiritual victory. He had somehow molded Morris and Theresa closer together than ever before as they sacrificed for the cause of Christ the very thing they had scrimped and saved for these past several years.

To everyone, it felt like Christmas.

A wedding.

Easter.

Thanksgiving.

All rolled into these few precious moments.

As they drove home—together again as a family—heading towards their rented apartment, Morris and

Theresa had no way of knowing that God was already pouring out His blessings on their lives from the heavens.

God was already providing a way for them to buy the very same house they had given up for the people of Greece, one year later, at precisely the same price they were going to buy it for before Morris left on his historic crusade.

God would restore the downpayment, and give them back the very same house they had given to Him.

Within twelve months, Morris Cerullo would be busy building a study downstairs. Theresa would be busy sewing, making matching bedspreads and draperies for the kids' rooms from fabric she bought at the local discount store.

They gave their house to the Lord and used that money to finance Morris's first overseas crusade, and one year later, God gave that home back to them.

But none of that mattered on this evening as the four Cerullos motored home from the airport.

The only thing that mattered now was that they were at last together again.

CHAPTER FOURTEEN

VOODOO VANQUISHED IN HAITI

For the next several years, the Cerullo family conducted the clerical functions of the ministry out of the garage of their home. Even little Mark, the newest Cerullo son, although only four years old in 1960, had his assigned ministry tasks.

Only the family car was left out of the constant activity. Since Morris Cerullo traveled more now to the foreign nations of the world, it often sat parked in the street.

The Cerullo family answered their correspondence on an old wooden table with a crickety manual typewriter whose keys hit each other if you typed too fast. The children learned the joy and privilege of doing God's work, and each child helped after school and at nights. Sometimes they would lick the envelopes. Sometimes they would fold the letters and stuff them. Sometimes they would empty the trash. But all the family members contributed.

Since that historic first crusade in Greece, Daddy was now regularly going to the foreign fields, reluctantly leaving his wife and family behind.

In these past few years, Morris Cerullo had learned that

despite the differences in religion, the existence of cults, despite the political climate or governmental condition of any particular nation, the real battle he faced was always spiritual.

Before he ever stepped on to a crusade platform, before he uttered one word to the awaiting crowds, he had already taken the spiritual authority and control away from the enemy through hours—sometimes days—of intense prayer and spiritual warfare. It seemed all the devil could do in a Morris Cerullo crusade or meeting was poke up his ugly head once in awhile and cause a little commotion here or there before retreating.

However, in the Haiti crusade of 1960, the devil apparently decided to pull out all the stops and wage a powerful, full-scale offensive against the twenty-nine-year-old evangelist. The territory and the timing of the warfare were clearly weighted in Satan's favor.

The ensuing spiritual battle I'm about to relate to you is absolutely true. There were thousands of witnesses. And when the final course of spiritual history is written in the books of heaven, Morris Cerullo's battle in Haiti may prove to be one of the classic engagements of spiritual warfare in our generation.

*   *   *

The open door to journey to Haiti, a nation enmeshed in the practice of voodoo, came from a personal invitation from Demos Shakarian, founder and president of the Full Gospel Business Men's Fellowship International, a world-wide outreach to men based in Costa Mesa, California.

Demos challenged Morris Cerullo to develop spiritual battle plans for a series of hard-hitting crusades with FGBMFI to penetrate the island of Haiti for the cause of Christ.

Morris immediately accepted the challenge.

The crusade's timing could not have played more perfectly into the devil's plan. The FGBMFI organizers booked the stadium during Haiti's annual Mardi Gras celebration, a festival dominated by lust, sexual perversion, rape, drunkenness and voodoo.

By the time Morris arrived, posters advertising the Christian crusade had either been burned publicly or remained prominently displayed with voodoo pins piercing Morris Cerullo's picture.

Mardi Gras in Haiti in 1960 was unlike any other celebration in the world. The activities took place on seven consecutive Sunday nights and were the wildest, most ungodly displays of carnality you could ever imagine. Almost a hundred thousand people were out on the streets in Port-au-Prince, the site of the Cerullo crusades, for those Sunday nights, reveling, drinking, engaging in all sorts of open sexual expression, and gaudy, sometimes bloody displays of vile voodoo rites at every street corner.

Truly, this was the devil's day! The local newspapers reported that during the first three Sunday nights of the pagan celebration, thousands of women of all ages were openly raped, with no interference from the local police officials.

The ministry team arrived in Haiti on the third Sunday of the Mardi Gras season. They immediately learned that although eighty percent of Haiti is reportedly Catholic, the strong influences of African voodoo permeate every part of the island. Many Catholics attended Sunday mass in the morning, then enthusiastically participated in the pagan Mardi Gras rites at night!

Naturally, the local witch doctors of Port-au-Prince considered Mardi Gras *their* season. They strongly resented the publicity, announcements and distractions of the Cerullo crusade. Some of them decided to create a volatile, hostile situation at the upcoming crusade to teach this young American evangelist a lesson he'd not soon forget.

*   *   *

The air was electric at the stadium in Haiti as the time drew ominously near for the opening service of the crusade.

President Francois Duvalier himself, Haiti's dictator, had invited the FGBMFI and Morris Cerullo to come to his country. So out of respect to President Duvalier, almost two hundred dignitaries and high-ranking military officials, many of them Catholic, sat on the platform with their wives as the crusade opened.

The platform was erected in the middle of the stadium floor, and five thousand people were jammed around the platform, standing in the open area. Another ten thousand people were packed into the stands. Many were laughing, jeering and mocking.

Scattered throughout the crowd were three hundred red-shirted Haitian voodoo witch doctors. They came to to create havoc, to wreck the platform, and possibly even to kill whomever would dare interfere with their evil purposes. Their prime target was Morris Cerullo, the featured evangelist.

As the Christian leaders with whom Morris was making the trip sought to open the meeting and give their personal testimonies, the voodoo witch doctors began their rhythmic disruption and chanting.

Boom.

Boom.

Boom.

Boom.

These enemy warriors started to march defiantly around that platform positioned in the middle of the stadium field. The Christians and dignitaries on the platform seemed stranded on a tiny island surrounded by hostile sharks anxious to harm their prey. Morris Cerullo recognized that Satan had fully unleashed a host of evil spirits against this mighty work of God.

*　　　*　　　*

A few hours earlier, when he had arrived in Haiti, a long string of limousines waited to take him and the other Americans on a parade through the city before arriving at the hotel. Morris Cerullo was in a car with several high ranking government officials, including Senator Arthur Bonhomme and a general.

At the time, Morris knew little about the spiritual habits of Haiti. But in his spirit, he sensed that something different was about to happen. The very air smelled sickening. Vile. He felt a lingering sickness in the pit of his stomach, and turned to his hosts and said, "Please pull this car out of the motorcade."

"What do you mean?" his official hosts asked, quite surprised by the request. "We can't pull out. We are going to take you by the President's palace!"

"I can't tell you why," Morris responded, knowing the Lord was clearly speaking to him, "but I must get to my hotel now."

The authority in the young evangelist's voice overcame the pageantry and the preconceived plans. Still confused, but without any further questions, his Haitian hosts dropped Morris Cerullo off at the hotel and attended to his room reservation. As soon as he entered his room, without even taking the time to unpack his bags, he immediately got down on his knees and began to pray.

"God," he began, "something's wrong here. This is not a sickness. This is a spiritual thing. You're wanting to speak to me."

And he was right. The Lord spoke to him, not in an audible voice, but in his spirit.

"God," he said aloud, "what's wrong?"

The answer came readily back. "Tonight there are going to be three hundred witch doctors at the crusade. You'll know them because they will wear red shirts. They're going to scatter themselves throughout this congregation, and they're there for the purpose of killing you. They're going to come out to kill you," God said to Morris.

"Lord," he said, "thank you for telling me. I don't mind being a martyr if you want me to die."

In his short life-span of twenty-nine years, he had already faced about everything there was to face, so he prayed, "Lord, if you want me to, I'll die." He meant it.

Then God said, "Son, I want you to remember something when you are out there tonight. The words you speak will be exactly as if I had spoken them and I will bring the words to pass."

*   *   *

Fear. The local ministers radiated fear. They believed they knew the power of the witch doctors, and had heard of their plans to disrupt and destroy the evening meeting. So these well-intentioned pastors came to Morris Cerullo at his hotel and presented their plea.

"Now, Brother Cerullo, we don't want to tell you what to do. After all, you are the man of God. But, we do not want to encourage you to have a Sunday night meeting.

"Of course, if you do, those of us in the churches will come, but you should know that a Sunday night meeting will conflict with the Mardi Gras celebration. Here in

Haiti, that is the most important festival of the year.

"We think you would be well-advised not to have a Sunday night meeting. The witch doctors do not like it and they will march against you. They will burn you in effigy and put pins in your pictures while they perform their voodoo dances. Already, they are calling their evil spirits down on you."

One man present at that meeting was C.C. Ford, one of the executive directors of the Full Gospel Businessmen, and a personal friend of Morris Cerullo. Mr. Ford understood the spiritual authority that Morris represented and spoke up in answer to these trembling pastors before Morris could reply. His answer spoke succinctly for the prophet.

"Let me tell you something about Brother Cerullo," Mr. Ford replied confidently, "one thing about him you will come to understand is that he is not consecrated unto life, he is consecrated unto death. He has no fear of death nor of your witch doctors."

And that was the end of the discussion. Clearly, the Sunday night meeting would take place as planned.

*   *   *

The voodoo chants chilled the crowd. The electric atmosphere generated fear. Even the government officials and military officers sitting on the platform behind Morris Cerullo felt the fire of voodoo frenzy, and they anticipated a riot.

Cerullo began to speak. Every time he'd start to talk, the witch doctors would start that chant again.

Boom.

Boom.

Boom.

Boom.

The emotions of the crazed crowd skyrocketed with each beat of the hateful chant.

From all parts of the stadium, witch doctors and voodoo supporters poured out of the stands and marched around the platform.

The platform started to shake as the mass of humanity now marching around it rocked the very foundation.

It seemed that at any minute the red shirts would rush against the platform, tear it down, and then kill God's man, Morris Cerullo, to prove once-and-for-all the force of their voodoo power.

Morris Cerullo turned around for his interpreter who was a Bible school boy named Nelson. Pointing his finger sternly at him, he said, "Son, I want you to interpret what I say—*every word*. Don't you dare change a single word. Not one syllable."

"Yes, sir! Yes, sir! Yes, sir! " Nelson agreed, too frightened to think.

The man of God once again called for the attention of the frenzied crowd, and began.

"God, the *true* God, has sent me to Haiti," he declared boldly. "The devil, who is against God, wants to keep you in bondage. He has sent these hundreds of voodoo witch doctors here tonight to try to kill me and destroy this meeting."

Several times, Morris Cerullo called for quiet, but to no avail.

Finally, with the authority of the Holy Spirit, the evangelist charged, "Today, in my room, God showed me that there would be hundreds of red-shirted witch doctors here tonight to destroy this meeting. But I am going to be in this city for some time. So, we'd better find out tonight, this first night, whether you and your devil have more power than me and my God!

144

"We're going to find out right here tonight who has the greater power, the living God whom I serve, or the devil, who sent these witch doctors."

The booms stopped. The chanting ceased. Morris Cerullo now had their complete attention.

"The God that I came here to tell you about is a loving God. He sent me here to tell you that He loves you so much that He wants to take away all of your sins, take away your burdens, and yes, even take away your sicknesses. I've come here to tell you how you can be free of all those things."

He paused just long enough to make the enemy uncomfortable. Then he continued.

"But that God is a God of judgment.

"The next witch doctor, or any person who opens his mouth to destroy this meeting in any way, shape, or form, before all these officials," and he gestured to all the dignitaries sitting on the platform, "well, I will not be responsible for that person when they carry you out of this stadium dead."

Morris Cerullo turned to the dignitaries on the platform and repeated his words, knowing that he was under God's anointing, and that God had already promised him that whatever words he spoke that night in the crusade would be honored.

"The next person on these grounds, and in this stadium, who opens his mouth and says one word to hinder or destroy this meeting, I will take no responsibility before all you officials, when they carry that person out of this stadium dead!"

There was absolute stillness.

Not even the witch doctors appeared ready to challenge the God of the young evangelist.

For about the next twenty minutes, Morris spoke

without interference when suddenly, behind the field crowd of five thousand standing before the platform, somebody began to scream.

But it was not a witch doctor trying to disrupt the meeting. Instead, a group of Haitians started to push a small baby girl toward the platform, moving her with their hands above their heads. The people were so packed together that if one of them moved, all of them moved. The whole crowd seemed to be swaying back and forth, side by side, as they passed the baby along, overhead, toward the platform.

Someone began to scream, "Reverend Cerullo, this baby was born blind, and now it can see. She sees!"

A different sort of frenzy broke upon the meeting— the same kind of frenzy, the same type of joy that must have hit the apostles on that first Pentecost.

Everybody was yelling and crying while they passed the child towards the platform. A government official stood up, dressed in the uniform of a soldier with a high rank. He stood there with his hands up over his head, looking in astonishment at that baby girl.

He shook with emotion.

"Mr. Cerullo," he whispered hoarsely. "Mr. Cerullo, that's my neighbor! That baby is my neighbor." And then the crowd went wild.

When the little girl finally arrived in front, Morris Cerullo began to verify the miracle.

"How do you know this baby was born blind?" he asked to those in the audience. "Are the parents here? If they are, let them through."

The stadium held thirty-five thousand people and five thousand of them were jammed right smack up against that platform in the middle of the field. But somehow, the parents pushed their way through the crowd. The mother and father came up on the platform to be with their little baby.

As they held her, the little girl grabbed at Morris Cerullo's white handkerchief, at his nose and ear, and followed every movement on the stage with her newly functional eyes.

Her eyes followed flawlessly as Morris Cerullo shifted from spot to spot. It was true! This baby, that had been born blind, was now seeing for the first time! The entire audience was electrified.

The leading witch doctors who only moments ago plotted the death of Morris Cerullo now fell to their knees and gave their lives to Jesus Christ, accepting Him as their Savior.

The crusade exploded in an endless display of ministry and miracles. Before the meeting was adjourned, the defeat of the devil was complete and total.

That night, when Morris went back to the hotel, his entire being basked in the afterglow of God's power. His sense of satisfaction was overwhelming. Thousands of people had yielded their lives to Jesus under the anointing of the Holy Spirit.

As Morris pulled his exhausted body into bed, he humbly thanked the Lord in simple prayer for anointing him as a chosen warrior, and for allowing him to be His faithful servant.

*   *   *

The crusades lasted three weeks, instead of five days as planned.

The crowds swelled consistently to over thirty-five thousand daily. Thousands were saved, healed and received the ministry of the Holy Spirit.

Hundreds of witch doctors were saved. During the three weeks, thousands of voodoo fetishes were brought and piled on the altar to be forever destroyed!

The leading witch doctor of the whole city of Port-au-Prince received Jesus Christ as his personal Savior and even invited Morris and many of the local ministers to come to his home.

This witch doctor then did an amazing thing to testify to the sincerity of his born-again experience. He took the ministers on a tour of every room in his house and started handing his once-treasured voodoo fetishes to Morris and the pastors.

Then, they assembled in the street, and there, in full view of the witch doctor's neighbors, they dumped the fetishes in a huge pile, took a torch to them, and set them ablaze.

Morris Cerullo and the other ministers stood proudly out in that street, in front of that witch doctor's whole neighborhood, with tears in their eyes, singing, "What can wash away my sins, nothing but the blood of Jesus."

*   *   *

After the second week of crusades, the Haitian Mardi Gras died.

Where there were normally about a hundred thousand people dancing crazily in the streets, you could only find about thousand people carousing.

The rapes and drunkenness had virtually stopped.

Instead of the night air smelling of the newly sacrificed blood of animals, Haiti had instead been cleansed and purified by the blood of Jesus.

The revelers now attended the meetings.

One night, Morris Cerullo gave an altar call just for men, and out of that packed stadium, about fifteen thousand men came down out of the stands and gave their lives to Jesus.

The victorious evangelist, exercising the divine

anointing and authority God had given to him, commanded and commissioned these men to live holy lives. To go home and repent of their sins. To ask forgiveness of their wives for their infidelity and their adultery.

This historic spiritual event helped many island men, who were involved sexually with women other than their wives, to repent of their infidelity and to become good husbands.

As the plane lifted off from the Haitian runway to return Morris Cerullo back to the United States and his precious family, even the usually stale air in the plane cabin seemed refreshingly clean.

A monumental spiritual battle had shaken the very heart and soul of Haiti, and the results of that clash had a significant positive effect on the spiritual history of that tiny island nation.

CHAPTER FIFTEEN

HOMECOMING AND HEARTACHES

While driving to the airport to meet her returning husband, Theresa was thinking to herself, "I never get used to Morris leaving for weeks at a time. God, I miss him. The best part about his trips overseas is now, when I drive to the airport to pick him up."

Mark, Susan and David were all struggling to keep their eyes open. They were already dressed in pajamas, robes and slippers, since the plane would not arrive until late. On this particular trip to the San Diego airport to pick up her husband from his crusade in Brazil, only Theresa was wide awake.

The year was 1962, and Morris had now been traveling to the foreign fields fairly regularly for seven years. Yet, the welcome home greetings were always special.

As Morris met the family in the airport, and after the first emotions, warm hugs, kisses, and tears were over, Theresa noticed that her husband's face was somehow different. She could always tell when something special was on his mind.

"Honey, what is it?" she asked as she walked arm in arm with her Morris to the car.

"After we get the kids home and tucked in to bed," Morris said, "I'll tell you. It's too complicated to share right now with all the commotion from the kids."

That night, after David, Susan and Mark were gently tucked in to bed, and after Morris and Theresa read to them out of scripture, the parents went into the kitchen where Morris shared with her one of the most incredible incidents his lovely young wife had ever heard.

*   *   *

"Honey, the turnout for the crusade in Porto Alegre, Brazil, was everything we had hoped and prayed for. At least fifty thousand people jammed into the Exposition Grounds. But when I started to minister—in fact, I'd only been speaking for about ten minutes, a tremendous pain suddenly shot across my chest."

"Oh, Morris," Theresa said, concerned about her husband, "why didn't you call and tell me? Was it your heart?"

"At first I thought it might be," Morris replied. "I had the horrific thought that here I was, only thirty years old, and already suffering a heart attack. I can tell you this, Theresa, it hurt so much that I grabbed the thin board railing on that platform. It wasn't very substantial, but I grabbed for it and held on. My whole body was doubled over with pain. The pain shot across my chest like this," and he motioned to Theresa that the pain had traveled from the left to the right side of his chest.

Theresa slid a bit closer to him and hugged his hand as she listened attentively.

"I asked the Lord, 'Am I going to die? God, are you going to take me home now?' I was collapsing in the pulpit from the excruciating stabs in my chest. I pulled my overseas director to the microphone and told him to close the service so I could get into the automobile parked behind the platform and have it take me back to the hotel.

"By then, Theresa, my entire body was so exhausted that I literally fell limp into the back seat."

"Then what happened?" she asked. "Did you tell the driver to immediately take you to the hospital?"

"No, I didn't want him or anybody else to know what was happening. So, I just told the driver to get me back to my hotel room.

"On the entire drive back to the Plaza, the pain continued. I staggered to get on the elevator and I stumbled to get to my room. I was in such pain when I got there that I didn't even take the time to remove my clothes, which were soaking wet from perspiration. Theresa, it must have been 105 or 110 degrees on the platform that night. Even my shoes were sopping wet."

She caressed his arm a little tighter and gently squeezed his hand as she listened.

"I remember I had a very hard time even falling down on the floor to pray," Morris continued, "because my room was so small."

"I thought the name, 'Plaza Hotel' sounded so fancy," Theresa interrupted. "You mean your room was as bad as some we stayed in during our crusade travels?"

"Yes, it was very small, and not fancy at all. It was located right smack in the heart of downtown. I could hear a lot of street noises. Right across the street was a little park where people would walk around, like a promenade. It was terribly noisy. Honking trucks. But God didn't care about those physical circumstances. He spoke to me in spite of all of that."

"Did He speak to you right away?" Theresa wanted to know.

"Yes, just as soon as I fell on the carpet on my face

before God. I prayed, 'Lord are You taking me home?' God immediately let me know that this pain was not for the purpose of Him taking me home to heaven. In fact, as I lay there, the pain lifted completely and it has stayed away. Theresa, I feel great now.''

''I'm so glad. What a relief,'' Theresa sighed, hugging her husband as he continued.

''As I realized the pain was gone, God came into my room and He spoke very clearly and very directly to me. He said, 'Son, I have permitted this to happen to you for a purpose.' I said, 'Lord, please teach me.'

''Theresa, you know it is very scary to think your life is over at thirty, especially at a time when God seems to be blessing our ministry outreach in an explosive and miraculous way.''

''I don't believe God would take you now either, Morris,'' the young wife replied confidently. ''He has too much work for you to do. So what did He say to your request that He teach you?''

''God asked me a very peculiar question. He said, 'Morris, what do you want out of this life?' I thought, 'It is very strange for God to ask me that.' ''

''Morris, that is strange,'' Theresa reacted. ''After all, God knows your heart and He knows mine. He knows us better than we know ourselves. You've traveled with me and the kids for five years. You've traveled on the foreign fields without us for seven. You've gone everywhere He's told you to go and done everything He's told you to do. Morris, our lives are totally on the altar now and always have been.

''Didn't that question surprise you?''

''Of course it did. In fact, I said, 'God, why would You ask me what I want most out of this life when you know the complete dedication and total consecration that I have made to You? Why would You ask me what I want most out of life?' "

"Morris, that's such a staggering question," Theresa responded after she had a few seconds to think about God's question. "It almost sounds like God asked You so He could grant you any desire of your heart. You could have probably asked for anything at that point and I believe God would have granted your request. So what did you tell Him you wanted most?"

"I told Him, 'Lord, there is only one thing that I ask of You in this world...only one thing,' and my answer came pouring out of my innermost being. 'God, give me the ability to take what you have given me, the power and anointing and the glory that is upon my ministry, that You have rested upon me and give me the ability to give that to others.' "

"Morris, I knew you would say something like that," Theresa replied. "That's been your heart ever since I've known you. We both know the only way we will ever reach this world for God is if God raises up trained and motivated women and men, full of the power of the Holy Spirit. These nationals can go the villages and country-sides of their own countries and evangelize their own nations."

"That's right, Theresa. The key is dedicated, trained, motivated nationals who can go into the highways and byways of their own countries with the message and the power of the resurrected Son of God. They can go places I can never go, often places no outsider could ever hope to reach."

"That's what makes your ministry so different," Theresa replied, even more excited. "The world will not be reached just through the full-time preachers and seminary students. It will take lay people—doctors, housewives, lawyers, grocers, nurses, farmers, full of the power of the Holy Spirit who can go back into their villages and their cities to evangelize their own nations."

"That's right, honey, I've said it a hundred times. Africans reaching Africans, Asians reaching Asians, South Americans reaching South Americans, until every continent and every nationality is saturated with the gospel of Jesus Christ."

"So what did God say when you told Him the desire of your heart?"

"As I lay before God there on that hotel floor, God said to me..." and here Morris paused, deeply overwhelmed by the sacred and challenging words he was about to share..."Son, build Me an army!"

"Build Him an army?" Theresa questioned, not understanding the impact of the words. "What do you think He meant by that?"

"Well, at first I didn't totally understand.

"I walked around for days in prayer, asking God to help me see His plan. Now, Theresa, I believe the answer is clear. God Himself has given us our ministry marching orders! I believe those moments on the floor in the Plaza Hotel in Porte Alegre, Brazil, will forever change the course of our global evangelism efforts.

"God's crystal-clear purpose for my life is to *build Him an army of nationals.*"

Morris paused to wipe a tear from his eye, then he continued.

"Honey, the concept is exploding in my spirit even as I share it with you now. He has appointed me as His spiritual general to travel to the nations of the world and enlist recruits for life-long service. He has commissioned me to build Him an army of trained, motivated soldiers to win the world for Jesus Christ."

"Now I am starting to understand it a bit more clearly," Theresa replied, growing more excited. "In a natural army, you recruit people. So God wants you to recruit nationals to join His army, and after you recruit them, He wants you to put them into some sort of a spiritual bootcamp where you can demonstrate to them how to use the spiritual ammunition God has given you to do His work."

"Well, that's close," Morris responded. "But it has to be more than that. It has got to be ongoing training. You see, if you were a natural army, how could you win a war if all you did was recruit, enlist, and put people through bootcamp and then hand them a powerful rifle and say 'Go get them'? No, it will take more than that. We must do ongoing training."

"How are we going to do that, Morris? You are only one man. These trips to the foreign fields are so demanding and time-consuming as it is."

"God will give us the wisdom and the strength to do it," Morris replied. "I believe He wants me to start some sort of National Training Institute to train nationals all around the world and to pass on to them the same proof-producing anointing that God has given to me.

"He wants me to demonstrate the power of God in the lives of others. These Nationals...God's Army... are the hope of our world."

"Do you think that's why God had us move to San Diego?" Theresa asked.

"Honey, I'm sure of it. He was positioning us for His next major outreach to reach the world for the cause of Christ."

"Daddy, can I have a drink of water?" Mark asked as he sleepily walked into the kitchen.

"Well of course you can," Theresa replied, getting up

to get Mark a glass of water. After she filled the glass, she paused, looked at Morris, and smiled. Then she walked over and handed the glass to Daddy.

"Come here, son, here's your water," Morris answered, and patted his youngest son on the head as he drank every drop.

"Good night, Daddy," Mark said, hugging his dad and heading off to bed.

"Good night, Mark," Theresa and Morris both replied in unison.

"It sure feels good to have him home again," Theresa thought as she turned off the kitchen light and the couple went off to bed.

SECTION FOUR

ENDTIME EXPLOSION

CHAPTER SIXTEEN

THE MYSTERY OF MAGNITUDE

In these past fifty years, there have been more inventions, more discoveries and more scientific and medical breakthroughs than in the entire history of the world. And modern science is predicting that before the end of the twentieth century, we will see more inventions, more discoveries and more explosive breakthroughs in science, medicine, communication technologies and in space exploration developments than in the entire known history of humankind!

Our total knowledge will double in slightly more than one decade! Month after month, many technical breakthroughs are happening all around us so fast that they almost go unnoticed.

When a supercomputer nicknamed "Bubbles" made its debut in Minneapolis with a liquid-cooled memory, it could store more than two billion bytes of information and complete more than a billion computations per second. Before Bubbles was developed, the fastest computer known to man spewed out only two hundred million computations per second.

Bubbles was five times faster than any other computer

in the world—overnight—yet this amazing technological breakthrough barely made the local newspapers.

However, within a few months after Bubbles' introduction to the scientific community, other computers were introduced that just as suddenly dwarfed Bubbles' amazing computing abilities.

Imagine the impact on your own life if you woke up one morning and suddenly discovered that General Motors had invented a new gasoline engine capable of getting two hundred miles per gallon! That announcement would be like the breakthrough that Bubbles brought to the computer industry—overnight!

When the Wright brothers launched the first heavier-than-air machine on the sand dunes at Kitty Hawk, North Carolina, on December 17, 1903, the world stood in awe and amazement.

Yet only sixty-five years later, Neil A. Armstrong, an Apollo 11 astronaut, took a human's first step on the moon!

In 1903, the air transportation industry did not exist.

Today, it is not uncommon for business executives to accumulate one million miles of air travel with a single airline. Today, air passengers world-wide are counted in the billions.

In medicine, fertility clinics now have the ability to remove several eggs from an infertile woman, fertilize them, and then implant them months, even years later, by a freezing process.

This "new technology" may allow a sterile couple to produce children, but it brings with it huge complex legal and moral questions, questions man has never encountered before. These are not normal times. The daily breakthroughs continue.

The breakthroughs in satellite technology have literally

shrunk the world to the point where a media event can be seen and heard anywhere on earth in a matter of milliseconds.

Within one generation, a young boy who grew up listening to the marvels of a radio program is now a middle-aged man watching events unfold live, and in color.

The coronation of a queen continents away is beamed in seconds into living rooms everywhere. The nations of the world have literally become visitors in our homes.

CAT scanners almost make the internal workings of the human body visible and allow doctors to study any organ they desire—without X-rays.

Doppler Diagnosis allows blind people to see with sound. Solar-powered satellites now circle the earth. The magnitude and frequency of these incredible advancements in knowledge are paralleled by other areas of magnitude unique to this century.

There has been an unprecedented increase in population in our generation. Historically, disease and famine have always acted in a tragic, yet functional combination to control the world's population. Today, in the midst of the greatest diseases and the largest famines humanity has ever experienced, the population explosion is escalating.

During the ancient times of Jesus Christ, there were only an estimated two hundred fifty million people on the face of the earth. Sixteen centuries passed before that number doubled. When the Pilgrims landed at Plymouth Rock, there were about five hundred million people in the world. The world population was doubling about once every sixteen hundred years.

Shortly before the outbreak of the U.S. Civil War, one billion people inhabited our earth. That meant the population had doubled in two hundred years. The addition of successive half billions has required increasingly shorter time. The sixth half billion required slightly more than ten years. The eighth half billion took only seven years. The ninth took only six years.

The absolute increase of people just in the population of Latin America during the last half of this century may easily equal the total increase in the population of man since his origin until the year 1650.

At the current rate of growth, our world population will double every thirty-five years. By the end of this century, scientists are projecting a total population of over seven billion! More people than have ever lived in our history live today. The world continues to explode with people at an increase and a magnitude never before seen in history. Seventy million people are added to our world every year.

In the midst of this world with multiplying people and exploding technologies, a spiritual warrior named Morris Cerullo, alone one night, desperately sought God in prayer.

"Lord, how can we ever possibly reach, evangelize and train such a rapidly exploding world with the saving gospel of Jesus Christ?"

CHAPTER SEVENTEEN

BARRICADES, BISHOPS AND THE PIED PIPER

T he letter from Reverend Nils Ivan Kastberg invited Morris Cerullo to conduct a crusade in Rosario, Argentina, the second largest city in that nation. Morris had already been jailed twice in Argentina for preaching the gospel, once in Corrientes and again at Mar Del Plata.

Yet, he agreed to come.

The dates were set for November 13 to 20, 1966. A football stadium accommodating 80,000 people was secured, and a permit obtained. As the crusade drew nearer, organizers encountered some resistance in placing their ads in the newspapers and on the radio and TV. Finally, the private secretary of the Roman Catholic bishop in this predominantly Catholic nation went with the crusade staff to the TV and newspapers and personally recommended the acceptance of the paid advertising. For many of these media, it was the first non-denominational Christian advertising they had ever accepted. Through these ads, the whole city was alerted that the chosen warrior was bringing proof to the nation that Christ is alive.

At first, the police department had seemed cordial and

co-operative, but on Saturday a notice banning the meeting was issued to Reverend Kastberg, the local chairman. As their reason the police said that the crusade would be of such magnitude that they would be unable to handle the crowd.

After issuing the ban, the chief of police went into seclusion, leaving orders that under no circumstances could his ban be reversed. He dispatched forty police to keep the crowds away from the football stadium. The officers on duty for blocks around the crusade grounds were not in sympathy with their superior's actions, but had to enforce the orders not to permit anyone near the stadium.

People gathered at 9:30 a.m. for a crusade scheduled to start at 7:30 p.m. The crusade staff was told that if they spoke words of explanation to anyone about the closure of the meeting, they would be arrested.

Even though the staff had secured permits for the stadium and for the crusade, now at gun-point, they were ordered not to speak to anyone or to enter the grounds they had rented. In the United States, we claim our rights; however, at this time in Argentina, under military dictatorship, there were no rights to claim.

Negotiations with the acting chief were fruitless. He gave the staff a text to read to the people which said: "The official act announced for this date is canceled. We will try to get permission for the forthcoming days, but in the meantime, we ask you to co-operate and go home in peace."

When Morris arrived at the grounds, the taxi carrying him was stopped. When he attempted to walk towards the grounds, he was again stopped—at gun-point. Morris ignored the barricades and guns and marched through to the stadium gates. Much like the legendary Pied Piper, he led thousands of people from the surrounding area after him.

One word from Brother Cerullo could have caused a riot. Clearly, he was in charge. Crowds had come for healing and help, but their own countrymen were denying them the right to receive divine blessings.

About ten thousand people surrounded Morris. The officers were moved to tears by the needs and eagerness of the crowd. Morris also wept tears of compassion for the needs of the multitudes, but was not allowed to say a single word. High ranking officers stood within feet of him, sympathetic, yet firmly obeying the chief's command not to allow him to speak.

Here the chosen warrior faced a strategic decision. Speak up, get arrested, and bring things to a head, risking someone getting hurt; or go along with the request of the missionaries to acquiesce to the police order in the hope that the problem could be reconciled the next day.

There was no easy way out. Morris chose the difficult course of saying nothing and being taken away peacefully from the scene.

Back in the hotel room, Morris said to his friend and senior ministry associate: "Even if I do not preach here, the whole city has had a witness. My ministry is to give witness to these nations before the coming of the Lord. The city had already been bombarded with full page ads, over one hundred thirty thousand hand bills, thousands of posters and banners, and hundreds of TV and radio programs. The whole city is stirred. While the closing of this crusade is the work of the enemy, God will turn it into a miracle revival and a great victory for His glory."

While Morris was being whisked away from the grounds with a police escort, two Christian pastors milled among the crowd inviting them to their two churches, located some miles away. Reverend Andresen had a church which usually held between one hundred and two hundred people. Now it was packed with hundreds, every foot of standing room taken. That night hundreds gave their heart to Christ. Several who were deaf, dumb, and blind and others with tumors were healed.

The same was happening at the tent that had been pitched for the minister's institute. (Over fifty national pastors were here from all over Argentina). The tent designed to seat four hundred was packed with more than a thousand.

The miracle revival Morris had spoken about was already coming to pass, and Morris had not spoken a single word.

Angered by their apparent failure to shut down the meetings, the next day the police closed out the morning service. It now became clear that this was more than an attack on Morris, because he was not scheduled to speak. "Crowd control" was not the real concern of the authorities. This was an attack against Christians, a higher battle against principalities and powers, against wickedness in high places.

All day Monday the staff worked and prayed unceasingly, but were unable to reverse the decision. The local military commander refused to see them. They were told that while he was sympathetic with their cause, his hands were tied. Therefore, seeing them would be to no purpose.

In an audience with the substitute chief, Morris gave the man an anointed witness. Moved, and with a tear in his eye, he said, "If it were in my power, you could have your meeting. I will take your cause to the chief with a positive recommendation. In less than an hour he returned to say that the chief was unwilling to reverse his previous order.

Monday night, Dr. Ness tried to go to the crusade grounds again, but the police with reinforcements were located four blocks away and more, not permitting people to come near the stadium. His car was stopped, so Dr. Ness got out and started to walk to the grounds.

The police surrounded Reverend Andresen and forbade him to interpret, so Dr. Ness, in his limited Portuguese, proceeded with a loud voice to speak to these dear Spanish people.

"Friends, I do not know why, but Morris Cerullo is forbidden from holding a crusade at the stadium. Please know that he is praying for you, and is deeply concerned about your needs. There will be meetings at these two churches," and he gave the addresses where the meetings would be held. That night the churches were packed again.

Morris had not yet spoken a word, but an unprecedented revival had broken out in Argentina. Many public officials were sympathetic, but powerless to change the order. The judge of the city courts said: "We are under the rule of a new revolutionary power. While you have been done a great injustice in that you have been given no justifiable reason for such action, it simply means this: if I ruled in your favor, higher powers would overrule my decision. Our constitution has no meaning in that present powers do not have to abide by it, so a favorable ruling does not have to be honored."

Morris, though concerned about the future of the Christian leaders here, was also eager to enter the arena of battle. With the insistence of local pastors, he preached on Tuesday night.

Every pew and chair was taken. The people stood tightly packed in the church, with crowds on the street trying to see or hear the chosen warrior. The press from

169

Buenos Aires was there as well as local TV.

Morris preached with a mighty anointing, but made no reference to the local problem. Two or three inflammatory words would have sparked a riot. He spoke only of the love and forgiveness of Jesus Christ. The local press came out with a sympathetic report, the first unpaid write-up about Evangelicals in Rosario's history.

The reporters from Buenos Aires stayed for the whole service. When the altar call was made, up went their hands to receive Christ. Two deaf and dumb mutes were interviewed by the press after Morris demonstrated their healing during the service.

Rosario was the site of a spiritual powder keg of expectancy and faith. The city of almost two million inhabitants, ninety-four percent Italian and European background, heavily Catholic, had never heard or seen such a witness of resurrection healing power.

Sensing that a great victory had already been won, the churches being crowded and overflowing, many miracles happening daily, a witness already having been given to this city and nation, Morris felt that the first phase of his mission had been accomplished. The second phase was already being planned.

In the first phase, although the crusade was completely stopped and not one mass meeting at the stadium was permitted, God had prevailed. Precious spiritual seeds remained in Rosario, growing before the next outreach.

Morris went back in February, 1967, three months after the first Rosario crusade.

*   *   *

There had been one hundred straight days and nights of prayer revival in Rosario when the crusade team arrived. It had been necessary to conduct four pre-crusade services each day in the churches to accommodate the crowds. One church that had numbered sixty-five before the first Morris Cerullo visit had now grown to eight hundred baptized members, with over four hundred awaiting baptism.

In just three months, a small, downcast group of despised believers had become a dynamic force in the community. Reverend Kastberg, who previously had to beg officials for the slightest concessions, was now treated with the utmost respect. The whole city was being transformed.

*   *   *

Thursday morning broke across the fertile rich farmlands of Argentina to what appeared to be the beginning of a perfect day. Not a cloud in the sky and the air was warm and fresh. But suddenly out of nowhere clouds appeared, and by 10:00 a.m. it began to rain, gradually increasing throughout the day until the streets were flooded with water. Work had to stop on the platform that was being constructed. The public address system could not be tested and checked.

At 4:30 p.m., the first break in the weather appeared. Those who were able to reach the grounds came. However, with many unpaved streets in Rosario, it made it impossible for most of the city to move for hours after the rain had stopped. About four thousand braved the hazardous travel to attend that first service.

Morris came to the microphone. Eggs and some small stones started to fly from a group nearby. Morris ignored them, and moved right into ministering under the anointing power of God. Soon, all of these fellows had dropped their stones and clubs.

Official government and medical observers were there scrutinizing every move and word. Prayer for the deaf and dumb brought an immediate response of miracles from every direction. Armenia Salazar had had a constant ringing in her ears for four years, which had kept her in continual torment. But now the noise had vanished. Armena Maroeflos had been totally deaf. Her ears popped open.

Many miracles happened that night, and with Friday having perfect weather, a much larger crowd could be expected for the evening crusade. But another type of cloud began to form.

Since the revival had broken out in Rosario, the previous church facilities had become totally inadequate, and even the tent could not serve the crowds that were coming. A beautiful theater with a capacity of twenty-five hundred had become available and had been leased for the morning services. When the staff arrived at the theater at 9 a.m. on Friday morning, they found that police officials had forbidden the owner to open the door, threatening him with arrest.

Reverend Kastberg went into immediate action. Three months ago his hands would have been tied, but now it was different. Even the police chief recognized the tremendous growth in the local churches these past three months. Within a half hour, officials withdrew the ban and the people streamed into the morning class.

The Friday evening crusade swelled to over twenty-five thousand people. The local College of Medical Doctors attended and they brought a district judge with them, hoping to discover a way to stop the meeting. Many more uniformed policemen were in evidence.

Never had the pastors and missionaries seen such a demonstration of the gift of wisdom in operation as they did that night. Every word Morris spoke seemed to come direct from heaven. The doctors became frustrated in their attempts to find grounds for arrest. The opposition had been staggered by the impact of the Word.

Testimonies began to flow across the platform. A five-year-old Catholic boy had had a large lump about the size of a man's fist since he was born and it instantly disappeared. His mother, Eva Pelote, could barely contain herself. After leaving the platform, they were immediately questioned by the magistrate.

Margarita Eva Bergara came to tell what Jesus had done for her. Margarita was a familiar sight at the stadium, because her father was the resident caretaker. She lived with her mother, father, six sisters and four brothers in three small rooms under the stands, just behind the platform. She had been choked by a goiter for more than four years. It had grown to the size of a large peach, causing extreme pain every time she swallowed.

As she stood in prayer, she felt something in her throat begin to slip down through her chest. She felt an emptiness in her throat. She swallowed and there was not the slightest pain. The audience stood to praise Jesus as if struck by lightning.

*   *   *

On Saturday night Morris arrived at the stadium just after the lights had been turned out by the police. There were dozens of army half trucks carrying soldiers who were armed with machine guns.

Crusade workers raced for the portable generator that had been brought to the soccer stadium in case of an emergency. But the police commissioner had anticipated the portable electric unit, for an armed policemen arrived at the generator simultaneously with the workers. He warned them, "If you touch this generator, you will be subject to immediate arrest and imprisonment."

The injunction to stop the meeting had not even been issued by the judge until 7:00 p.m. that evening. By that

173

time, tens of thousands had already come through the stadium gates. But now the gates were closed, and thousands of people coming from all parts of this metropolis and the surrounding countryside had to be turned away.

Almost total darkness.

No loudspeakers.

The police scattered to disperse the crowd.

When Morris arrived, he got out of the car and said, "Just follow me." Somebody said, "There's Morris Cerullo," and people broke through the barricades. Ten thousand people followed him down the street right to the front of the stadium.

As Morris attempted to enter, a policeman barred the way. Morris produced the permit signed by the chief of police, but this meant nothing. Immediately Morris realized that it was fruitless to plead his case on a lower level. Permits and constitutional laws mean nothing if a high government authority has sent down an order. The local police authorities, many of whom were very capable, intelligent men, looked embarrassed as they were forced to carry out orders that were contrary to justice. Morris was ordered to appear immediately at the police station or be faced with imprisonment for ignoring a summons.

Before he left, the chosen warrior stood on a car with a little megaphone and talked to the people, advising them to go to the church location that had been secured.

As a result of his evangelistic activities, Morris was arrested in Rosario, appeared before the magistrate, and for a short time was put in jail.

When he appeared before the judge, Morris shared with him God's master plan for the ages and when he was finished, the judge quietly bowed his head and said, "Let this man go free."

CHAPTER EIGHTEEN

CHOSEN PEOPLE, CHOSEN WARRIOR

D espite thirty years of anti-Semitic activity in Russia, on May 14, 1947, Andrei Gromyko, the Russian ambassador to the United Nations, under the direct orders of Joseph Stalin, gave a powerful speech to the special General Assembly session of the United Nations.

In that inspirational speech, Gromyko boldly declared that the Jewish people had experienced "exceptional sorrow and suffering" during World War II. He declared emphatically that "the time has come to help these people, not by word, but by deeds."

The Arabs were shocked by the unexpected reversal in the Soviet position. The Jews were confused, but grateful, for this unlikely and unexplainable Russian friend. In the months that followed, at virtually every step of the debate, the Soviet Union supported the Jewish position on the establishment of an Israeli state.

When the time came for the final vote on the issue of Israel as a nation, the entire communist bloc voted in favor of the Jews.

In 1948, after the atrocities experienced at the hands of the Nazi regime in Germany, the Jews recognized that the world was ready to restore Israel as a nation.

On May 14, 1948, a Jewish leader named David Ben-Gurion stood before a select gathering of two hundred people and declared:

"By virtue of the natural and historic right of the Jewish people and of the Resolution of the General Assembly of the United Nations assembly, we hereby proclaim the establishment of the Jewish state in Palestine to be called Israel."

The event marked one of the greatest miracles in history, one that astounded the world, and one that continues to amaze the world on an ongoing basis.

And, the event also marked the direct and dramatic fulfillment of an ancient biblical prophecy.

"Who hath heard such a thing? who hath seen such things? Shall the earth be made to bring forth in one day? *or* shall a nation be born at once? for as soon as Zion travailed, she brought forth her children" (Isaiah 66:8).

Before the entire world, out of the heels of the Holocaust, following the defeat of Hitler's forces, following the discovery by American bulldozers of the graves in the valleys in Germany of six million Jewish bodies burned in incinerators, the grave of Israel opened up and brought forth a new nation, resurrected in might, and embraced and sanctioned by the United Nations.

This miracle resurrection from their historic graveyard of dead nations was also foretold in the ancient pages of scripture:

"So I prophesied as he commanded me, and the breath came into them, and they lived, and stood up upon their feet, an exceeding great army. Then he said unto me, Son of man, these bones are the whole house of Israel: behold, they say, Our bones are dried, and our hope is lost: we are cut off for our parts. Therefore prophesy and say unto them, Thus saith the Lord GOD; Behold, O my people, I will open your graves, and cause you to come up out of your graves, and bring you into the land of Israel" (Ezekiel 37:10).

1948 saw the "graves open" and two million Jews came from all around the world to their new land...by plane, by boat, by caravan, by donkey....many of them drawn by strange and mysterious influences that they did not fully comprehend.

These two million Jews came because a force far greater than themselves had set in motion a miracle migration before they were even born:

"Fear not: for I *am* with thee: I will bring thy seed from the east, and gather thee from the west; I will say to the north, Give up; and to the south, Keep not back: bring my sons from far, and my daughters from the ends of the earth" (Isaiah 43:5-6).

God had ordained that these four major geographical areas—North, South, East and West—would participate in the miracle migration to Israel.

After 1,878 years of world-wide dispersal, the Jews in 1948 were marching to the tune of a heavenly pied piper, mysteriously being lured by a strange force they did not understand into a desolate desert that seemed uninhabitable to re-establish their long-lost nation according to a series of prophetic scriptures which they did not believe.

When the new Jews began to settle, Israel started to blossom in the midst of the desert.

"He shall cause them that come of Jacob to take root: Israel shall blossom and bud, and fill the face of the world with fruit" (Isaiah 27:6).

Israel is a nation birthed from the Jews of other nations. These Jews came from different backgrounds, spoke many different languages, and were even different colors.

The only thing these Jews had in common was their determination to make the tiny, new nation of Israel work in the middle of a parched land, barren and largely unsettled.

Over the following years and decades, the desert, once barren and supposedly unable to support life, started blooming everywhere as an incredible agricultural testimony of efficiency to other nations.

Yet another desert in Israel still remained. The spiritual desert. But in 1967, nineteen years after the re-establishment of Israel as a nation, God brought to His chosen people a chosen warrior, a warrior uniquely trained by Jewish rabbis to help his own people, the Jews, understand the scope of the divine destiny that has been theirs since the beginning of spiritual history.

The guiding hand that orchestrated the miracle migration of the Jews from around the world was now about to conduct a magnificent symphony of spiritual breakthroughs that would significantly influence Jewish history.

When the final pages of spiritual history concerning the Jews are written, they will say that "Morris Cerullo has strongly influenced the eternal aspects of Jewish history."

*   *   *

The bus bumped and bounced over the sometimes dirt, sometimes paved, always dusty road. Only the insufferable heat of the noonday sun attracted more attention than the ride itself.

Yet, in the midst of these distractions, Morris Cerullo was lost in his personal world of prayer to God.

This personal dialogue took place daily: on airplanes, cars, boats and buses. No matter where he was, or what

178

the mode of transportation, his intense prayer life separated him completely from physical distractions such as heat and dust.

For years, Morris had been praying, "Lord, since I have come to know Your Son Jesus as my personal Messiah, I feel an overwhelming burden to share the good news of salvation with my fellow Jews and with the nation of Israel. Lord, when will you allow me to go to Israel?"

Morris was a man of prayer and a warrior who obeyed his commander-in-chief. When told to go to Greece, he went to Greece. This was a general in God's army who recognized that no mission would be effective unless first ordered by the divine commander.

Although Morris had prayed this prayer for the Jewish people for years, he was a bit shocked that God deemed to pick this dusty bus in the middle of Argentina to grant his request. God spoke clearly to him.

"Son, turn your eyes to the Middle East, for now is the time to work for My people Israel." Morris bolted upright in the seat. For twenty years, Morris had waited, longing to hear those words. And now, the words of the psalmist that he had heard years ago could be applied in this instance:

"You will arise and have mercy on Zion; For the time to favor her, Yes, the set time, has come" (Psalm 102:13, NKJV).

Then God continued. "Son, do not be afraid. Go. I will open a door for you in Israel unlike any door I have ever opened."

Right there, riding on that bus in Argentina in 1967, Morris received from God the divine revelation on how to reach the Jews with the message of Jesus. He picked up a pen and began to write as God unfolded His Jewish outreach plan.

*　　　　　*　　　　　*

When Morris arrived back in the United States, the first thing he did was go to Israel where he published and mailed a Messianic booklet in Hebrew called "Besorat Shalom" (the gospel of peace) to twelve thousand Jews in Israel.

Over two thousand responses came in from that one mailing alone. But it was not enough. As Morris prayed about God's commission to reach every Jew, the Lord placed a question in his mind: "I wonder if there is a place that would list all the names of the Jews in Israel?"

A few days later, he obtained the name of a mailing house in Tel Aviv and drove over to see the owner. He plopped down his evangelistic literature on the owner's desk.

"Sir, I would like to mail this literature to whatever names you might be able to rent me."

"Who are you?" he asked.

"I am a Spirit-filled Jew," he said.

"What is a Spirit-filled Jew?"

Morris then explained what had happened to him in that Jewish orphanage at the age of fourteen and how he knew without a doubt that Jesus was the Messiah.

The old man browsed through the literature and then said, "Look, I'm a business man. I don't believe that religion should be governed by the state or anything else. If you want to mail this literature out, I will mail it for you."

They both signed the contract for a list of thirty thousand Jewish professional people, the only list the man had to rent.

Morris felt that was a good start, but knew in his heart that there must be something more.

As he was leaving, the man called him back.

"Mr. Cerullo, don't ask me why, but I have the feeling that I am supposed to do something else for you. How would you like to send your literature to every single home in Israel?"

Morris could not believe his ears. "I beg your pardon?"

The man continued, "I only have one list for rent, but I also manage and control the voter registration list of every Jew in the nation of Israel. There are over four hundred thousand names representing every household."

"I see," Morris replied, turning around and walking back to the man. "And how do I get permission to use this list?"

The answer Morris heard confirmed in his spirit the importance of the Jewish outreach and the divine hand of God guiding the master plan.

"Oh, I can give you permission to use the list. In fact, I will let you use it totally free of charge."

Morris tried hard to contain his excitement.

He wanted to jump up and down and shout "Praise the Lord," but he knew the man would not understand his enthusiasm.

"That's just great," Morris replied with some constraint.

Inside, his heart was leaping for joy. The list of every home in Israel...FREE! At that moment of excitement and amazement, the Holy Spirit spoke to him again: "Son, didn't I tell you I would open a door unlike any door I have ever opened?"

"Yes Lord, You did. You surely did."

*   *   *

The response to that massive mailing to four hundred thousand Jewish households was far beyond anything Morris and Theresa had ever dreamed. Thousands received Jesus as their Messiah. Soon, Morris Cerullo World

Evangelism was sending an Israel Bible Correspondence Course in Hebrew to over two thousand Jews and then to twenty thousand others who wanted to know the reality of their Messiah in a deeper, more personal way.

In 1975 and 1976, Morris produced, on location in Israel, the powerful and internationally acclaimed television drama, *Masada*. It was aired both in the United States and Canada. Nearly two hundred thousand persons responded, with many Jews coming to know Jesus Christ as Messiah from this media outreach.

In 1977, Morris mailed his powerful Jewish ministry outreach book, *Two Men from Eden*, to 3.2 million homes in North America. (If you would like a free, postage-paid copy of this very same book, write today to *Two Men from Eden*, Morris Cerullo World Evangelism, P.O. Box 700, San Diego, CA 92138).

At the conclusion of that book, there is a page that reads as follows:

A Challenge

MY COMMITMENT TO THE MESSIAH—JESUS!

This is to certify that on this date _____ I accept Jesus of Nazareth as my Messiah. I see in the Scriptures that He fulfills the prophecies spoken about the Messiah.

I accept Him as the Second Adam Who restores to me all the dominion and rights lost to me in the first Adam.

I do declare that Jesus is the living Messiah, the Son of God, and that through His Name I received the miracle of salvation, the gift of the new birth.

I believe He receives me now just as I am and gives me the power to become a child of God.

"And there is salvation in no one else; for there

is no other name under heaven that has been given among men, by which we must be saved" (Acts 4:12, NASB).

_____ Signed

_____ Date

In just one mailing alone, over ten thousand Jews signed, dated and returned this form, freely receiving Jesus as their Lord and Savior.

By 1978, the list of Jews receiving and completing the Israel Bible Correspondence Course had swelled steadily to over twenty thousand each issue!

Yet that was only the beginning of the Jewish outreach God had planned for the little Jewish preacher. Again and again, God miraculously opened doors to Israel far beyond that which any man could ever ask or think.

In the years since that first mailing, millions of pieces of literature have been distributed to Jews both in Israel and in North America. Thousands of Jewish people have recognized and received Jesus Christ as their Lord and Messiah through the ministry of the chosen warrior.

*   *   *

One of the directives God gave Morris Cerullo on the bus in Argentina was that he was to hold a Deeper Life Conference in Jerusalem. But that seemed an impossibility, because how could he find someone in Israel who would rent to Christians a place large enough for a convention?

One day, when he was at the King's Hotel in Jerusalem, Morris Cerullo saw a man Theresa and he had befriended in 1955.

"You used to be desk clerk here," Morris said. "What are you doing now?"

"Oh, I'm not the desk clerk anymore," the man

replied. "My brother and I own the hotel."

At that moment, Morris felt the direction of the Holy Spirit.

"I want to rent your hotel," he said. "I want to rent the kitchen, the dining room, every room—the whole hotel," he explained.

"You must be crazy," the Jewish owner replied. "What do you want it for?"

"I want to have a religious conference. You know that I'm an evangelist, and that I preach and pray for the sick and miracles take place. I want to have one of those ministry meetings here."

"I never heard of anything so ridiculous in my life," the hotel owner replied.

But then, almost as if he did not know why he was saying it, he continued. "But I will talk to my brother about it."

"All right," Morris said, "you talk to your brother and I will talk to my Partner."

"Is your partner in Jerusalem with you?" he asked.

"Yes," Morris replied, never telling the man that his Partner had been with him all the time.

The next day Morris's old friend still looked very puzzled.

"I don't understand it," he said. "I talked to my brother and he didn't think it was a crazy idea. We decided to rent you the hotel!"

Overnight God miraculously gave Morris a place to hold a Christian meeting in the heart of Israel.

In that first Israel Deeper Life Conference, at least 150 Jews were willing to risk the ridicule of their friends and the sanctions of their government, and publicly confessed Jesus as their Messiah.

Outside the hotel, Orthodox Jews demonstrated in

protest of the Christian meeting, but it continued until its planned conclusion.

*   *   *

Today, Morris Cerullo continues his rich, fulfilling outreach ministry to the Jews in Israel and in North America. He knows the divine task of introducing Jews to Jesus Christ as Savior has just begun.

After thousands of years of persecution, struggle and heartache, the vast majority of God's chosen people still cry out for peace. However, very few know the source of true peace: Jesus Christ, their Messiah.

The time for Jesus to be more fully revealed to His chosen people, the Jews, is here. Now is the set time to reach the Jews in Israel and North America for one purpose: to love them and to reveal to them through our lives and teachings that Jesus is their true Messiah.

God promises, "I will bless them that bless thee [Israel]," (Genesis 12:3).

Through a continuing ministry of conferences, literature, radio, films, TV and personal ministry, Morris Cerullo is committed to continue this outreach to God's chosen people until Jesus comes.

CHAPTER NINETEEN

TARGET: TANZANIA

In December, 1974, Tanzania was an African nation of thirteen million people and one hundred and twenty tribes. This fiercely nationalistic country located on the Indian Ocean, shunned every aspect of foreign influence in their culture. In an attempt to return to a pure African culture, clothing, music, and other fads from the West were strongly discouraged by the communist-influenced government.

It was in this political environment that Emmanuel Lazaro, the General Superintendent of the Assembly of God Churches in Tanzania, was placed in charge of the planning and preparations for the upcoming Morris Cerullo Crusade. As he made the initial plans, his frequent correspondence from Africa warned Morris Cerullo that this could be the last crusade allowed in Tanzania.

Due to heavy communist influence, the doors to religious freedom in Tanzania appeared to be closing.

*   *   *

Lowell Warner, a member of Morris Cerullo's crusade team, noticed that just two or three miles from the airport were a whole truckload of Communist Chinese workers coming down the road. He discovered that they were in the country to build the Trans-Zambian Railway. When he arrived at his hotel room, just outside of his window Lowell spotted a couple of very large Chinese passenger ships docked in the harbor, which were used for living quarters.

Lowell decided that it would be interesting to take a few pictures of Chinese communists working on an African railroad. But as he began to shoot the photos, he was immediately arrested and taken to the chief of police.

"Don't you know you cannot shoot pictures of our railway terminal?" asked the angry policeman.

"Of course I didn't know it was wrong," Lowell responded. "It seemed like a very normal thing to do to me."

Without responding, the Police Chief then told Lowell that they must now confiscate his camera and the film. But Lowell would hear of no such thing.

"What do you think the reaction of the American Press would be if I reported that I did not have the freedom in Tanzania to operate as a press photographer?" Lowell said. "How do you think it would look if I went back and told America that Tanzania does not have freedom of the press?"

After thinking about those remarks, the police chief decided to release Lowell, his camera, and his film. But the incident served as a warning about the intolerant Tanzanian political climate that the entire crusade staff was about to experience.

*　　　　*　　　　*

The city of Dar Es Salaam knew Morris Cerullo was coming to town because of the poster program. You could not go anywhere in town without seeing a poster plastered on the pillar of a downtown bar or tacked on the telephone pole in the business district. Walk a hundred yards in any direction and you would see five or six posters.

There were also newspaper advertisements, but they were restricted by the government. Everything in the newspapers had to be modified, so Morris Cerullo's usual copy concerning "The Blind Seeing, The Lame Walking, and The Deaf Hearing" was cut.

The location for Morris's first crusade and School of Ministry in Tanzania was a large athletic field six hundred yards square, used for military training from about noon to four o'clock each day. The city granted the staff permission to use the field, and a district officer gave Morris permission to hold the crusades on the grounds, not knowing that the spiritual training soon to begin would far exceed any military exercises these fields had ever seen in the natural realm.

On the first day of the crusade, Emmanuel Lazaro came running up to Lowell Warner and said, "The government is looking for me," he began, panting. "They want to close the meeting. What do we do?"

Lowell responded, "But you have a permit."

"Yes I do," Emmanuel said. "But in Tanzania, a permit does not make any difference. The government has changed its mind."

"Well, here's what you do," Lowell responded. "Emmanuel, you keep on the move so much that nobody can catch up with you. The rest of us will keep on working as though nothing is happening."

With that, Emmanuel left, and Lowell went back to work. The first night crowd was estimated to be about fifty-six thousand. As they flowed in, each person passed by dozens of army vehicles carrying armed soldiers.

When Morris prepares for a crusade, he always in-
structs his staff never to advise him of any political or
technical problems. He wants to concentrate solely on
what God would have him say. He relies on God to reveal
to him those things he needs to know.

As a result of this policy, when Morris arrived at the
Tanzania crusade and got out of his car, he was not aware
of the permit problem. The soldiers surrounded him immediately. They intended to stop Morris from going to
the platform. Their orders were clear and concise: "Do
not let this man preach."

When Morris got out of the car and saw these soldiers
running toward him, he stood at attention and gave them
his proudest military salute. The confused soldiers
stopped dead in their tracks. Then, they saluted him back.

As they saluted, Morris walked right past them. He
walked approximately one hundred yards across the field
to the platform. Around the edge of the platform were
more soldiers. He nodded to them as he went around
the side and ascended to the platform.

Dr. Ness had been given strict orders by the police that
under no circumstances was Morris to preach. But since
Morris knew of no such order, and since Dr. Ness was
not about to tell him, Morris stepped right up to the
microphone and began to preach.

Halfway through the service, four police cars came in
from the back of the grounds, followed by a paddy
wagon. As Morris was preaching, the police started coming toward the platform. Mac Nwulu from Aba, Nigeria,
went down to greet the policemen. They wanted to come
up on the platform and stop the meeting. But Mac said,
"No, you can't come up on the platform. This is only
for ministers up here. You can't come on the platform."

Mac radiated the spiritual authority that he had learned

190

from Morris. He just would not let the armed police come through the barrier. And so the police did not come up.

Instead, they stood and listened to the chosen warrior speak of the love of God, of the saving grace of Jesus Christ and of the forgiveness of sins. Before the service was over, these tough officers had removed their hats. Ninety per cent of them raised their hands in the air and accepted Jesus Christ as their savior. They had been commissioned to stop the man from preaching, yet that night the man preaching stopped them, and the grace of God had transformed their lives.

Scores of Muslims were healed from deafness, blindness and crippling diseases. After Morris finished praying for the sick, he left from a different direction from where the paddy wagon and the police cars were positioned. They had parked at the front gate; he departed through the back gate.

As the staff left the stadium, Lowell chuckled to himself while reflecting on how nothing ever seemed to phase Morris Cerullo. He remembered one time in India when a capacitor blew right out of the top of an amplifier about halfway through the service. Smoke was pouring out of the amplifier. Lowell walked up behind Morris and said, "The amplifier is blowing out. It's burning!" Morris just commenced to preach that much harder and went on preaching that much longer.

Later that night, the Tanzania police commissioner finally caught up with Morris's staff and explained that the crusade permit had been revoked. The government was not going to allow any more meetings.

"Why?" Morris asked.

"Because Tanzania is in a time of famine," was the reply, "and everyone is required to go home from work at 4 o'clock to prepare a plot for growing vegetables. This crusade is keeping the people away from the national program to raise more food. So we are going to close down the evening meetings and the school of evangelism.

"That won't do," said Morris. "Why don't we compromise? Why not let us hold the crusade tomorrow at the same location where the school of evangelism is?" Reluctantly, they agreed.

The next morning a new convert class was scheduled on the crusade grounds. The night before, it had been announced that all those who had accepted Christ could come back the next morning. When Dr. Ness arrived, there was a crowd of a couple of thousand people waiting. And three police cars. Five policemen stood on the platform, telling the people, "Everybody. No meetings. No meetings."

One black Muslim woman, dressed in black clothes, was in the middle of the crowd with her little boy who had been born deaf, dumb and blind. An army officer shoved her on the shoulder and said, "The meetings will not be held. You must disperse."

The woman stood up and announced, "You can drop a bomb on us if you want, but I am not moving. My son was healed last night, and I am going to stay here and wait for Morris Cerullo. Everyone in the entire street voiced their agreement. Nobody would move.

By 4 p.m., thousands of people had gathered. Despite the intimidation of the army, nobody would leave. The military officials finally approached Dr. Ness and said, "You have to say something because nobody will move."

Dr. Ness got up and explained that the crusade meeting had been canceled. Then he gave the location of the School of Ministry. In a great rush, the crowd took off and went to that place about a mile and a half from the crusade grounds.

When they came to the main boulevard, they just ran across the street and continued in a steady stream of people, blocking all traffic and city buses for about ten minutes.

Many Tanzanian ministers were intimidated by the police and wanted to cancel the School of Ministry. But Dr. Ness knew Morris would never agree to that, so he said to the ministers, "How is it going to look for Tanzania if all of the neighboring African countries send ministers and then they have to go back to their countries and say, "Well, look, we had no religious freedom whatsoever. They say there is religious freedom in Tanzania, but look, we could not even hold our minister's conference."

So, with the agreement of the local ministers, the second night of the crusade moved from the grounds to a rented auditorium that only held about two thousand people. Every seat was filled and thousands more stood outside.

Eventually, because of the crowds, the meeting moved to an Assemblies of God location twelve miles out of town that had a church and a fairly large lot. Tanzanian authorities allowed Morris to erect a platform, put up a PA system and lights.

Before this historic spiritual invasion in Tanzania there had been only one Christian meeting that had an attendance of two thousand people. The Morris Cerullo crusade was the only Christian event on a major scale that had ever taken place in Dar Es Salaam. If the crusade had not been stopped on the grounds, officials estimated that the crowds would have swollen to over one hundred thousand.

The chosen warrior literally opened Tanzania to the gospel and pioneered freedom of religion in that nation.

These meetings served to move Tanzania from only one hundred Christian churches to over one thousand in a few short years. A nation that shunned foreign influence had been touched and changed by the chosen warrior from America.

CHAPTER TWENTY

BALLOTS, BULLETS AND PRAYER

A single bullet is so small you can hold it in the palm of your hand. The raw manufacturing material costs about fifteen cents. The finished product weighs less than one ounce.

One bullet appears relatively harmless. But break through the brass casing of that bullet with the firing pin of a gun and the powder ignites an explosion, activating power. In its power-actuated state, traveling at over twenty-two hundred feet-per-second, that single bullet can change the course of an entire nation.

One bullet did just that on August 21, 1983, when it shattered the skull of Filipino opposition leader Benigno Aquino and killed him.

In just a few seconds, with only one bullet, the regime of President Ferdinand Marcos started to unravel. The entire tragic event was televised, from Aquino's arrest on the plane, to the actual recording of the sound of the shot, to the terrible sight of his body, dead, on the tarmac of the Manila airport.

Anti-Marcos riots and demonstrations broke out in the Philippine streets. Communist strategists came together, shouting, "Down with Marcos," and "Communism is the only hope of the oppressed masses." The political war in the Philippines escalated to a full-scale propaganda campaign with the lives of fifty-two million people depending on the outcome.

*   *   *

From April 27 to May 2, 1984, another event shook the Philippines and significantly altered the flow of that nation's spiritual history.

The Morris Cerullo School of Ministry activated a potent spiritual bullet, molded from the raw material of thousands of pastors and student leaders. This prayer-actuated group became empowered with the authority of Jesus Christ to become nation-changing proof producers in the Philippines.

When the school was scheduled to start, the vicious chants from anti-Marcos demonstrators rose above the noisy roar of downtown Manila. "Hitler. Marcos. Dictator. Dog." was their militant, bitter cry. A blood-red banner of the New People's Army, the military wing of the Philippine Communist Party, displayed a short but stern election message: STOP U.S. INTERVENTION IN THE PHILIPPINES.

In the thirty day period immediately before the spiritual invasion of God's Victorious Army for the Philippine School of Ministry in Manila, 399 Filipinos were murdered, primarily by members of the communist New People's Army, as the result of political tensions preceding the national elections. Young people searching for answers were easy prey to the growing communist movement in their changing country.

On election day, more than three hundred thousand soldiers and military police throughout the seven thousand islands which make up the Philippines were placed in the highest state of alert. Yet, fifty-seven Filipinos were still violently murdered while peacefully casting their vote at the polls. For the first time in his eighteen-year stint as president, the abusive government of Ferdinand Marcos was seriously challenged. The Filipinos were crying for the chance to govern themselves in political self-determination.

For decades, Morris Cerullo has taught the vital spiritual principle that ALL TRUTH IS PARALLEL, which means that what is going on in the natural realm will always be reflected in the spiritual realm as well. And that held true in 1984.

For hundreds of years missionaries had brought the gospel to the Philippines, but now, Morris knew it was time for the Filipino people to win their own nation for Jesus in a spiritual self-determination.

On April 27, 1984, when the Morris Cerullo World Evangelism School of Ministry opened in Manila, over 5,500 national leaders crammed the Philippine Plaza Convention Center to learn how to become soldiers for God. As they sat in rapt attention, Morris told them this dramatic story.

"Shortly after World War II," he began, "General Douglas MacArthur sent letters to scores of Mission Boards of various religious denominations around the world. He pleaded with them to send him ten thousand missionaries and he would give them a new Christian nation—Japan. The Japanese had viewed their Emperor Hirohito as a God; he was invincible. But when MacArthur's forces defeated the Japanese, they lost faith in their stone Buddhas and their emperor. Temples were empty. McArthur realized this, and sent letters to the missionary boards begging them to send him missionaries to Japan."

Here Morris paused, wiping a tear from his eye. His voice quivered as he spoke these next words.

"Of the scores of letters that he sent," he continued, obviously hurting deep from the inside at what he was about to say, "a total of three missionaries were sent by the boards. THREE. That's all they sent were three missionaries! McArthur received excuses like, 'We are not ready,' and 'We don't have the money'."

The thousands of students sitting in that room were absolutely quiet. Morris continued in a very hushed tone.

"Today, less than one-half of one percent of the people in Japan are Christians, because we failed to operate in God's spiritual timing."

Then, as if he were somehow miraculously infused with a tremendous shot of spiritual energy, Morris continued in a powerful and prophetic voice.

"Today, it is God's spiritual time for the Philippines," General Cerullo declared to his eager troops. "We failed God's timing for spiritual harvest in Japan. It was not long before the people began to return to their temples. They went back and worshiped their stone Buddhas and their pagan Gods. But today, we will not fail the Philippines. And today, we will not rely on missionaries from North America, but we will train and send *you*, the Philippine pastors and student leaders, to go forth and win your own country for Jesus Christ!"

The eager troops spontaneously stood up and enthusiastically saluted their general in a loud display of clapping and shouting.

Due to the overwhelming attendance, overcrowded registration lines required some students to stand for long hours, singing and praising the Lord. The main meeting hall held 4,250 people, but it was not large enough! Two over-flow rooms, each holding 550 students, were prepared and filled to capacity. The school doors opened each morning at 7:30 a.m., but the students were so anxious to hear their spiritual warfare instructors that they arrived before 6:00 a.m. each morning and waited patiently outside to get seats in the main auditorium. At lunch time, many students did not leave their seats for fear they would be occupied by someone else when they returned.

Several hundred people who were not registered for the school came and stood outside in the tropical heat, hoping to somehow absorb the school just by being near it. Morris requested a special loud-speaker be set up for these spiritual soldiers so they too could hear the biblical principles that have molded the ministry. Even in ninety percent humidity with temperatures well above one hundred degrees, these faithful troops joined in cheering and clapping along with the other students.

In the second teaching session, Brother Cerullo gave a prophecy from the Lord which brought the 5,500 Filipinos to their feet.

"The time has come for the Philippines to stop looking to America," he declared. "Keep your eyes off of politics. Stop worrying about the next move of the communists. When you know the truth about your God, then your hostile environment crumbles. God is going to have a people, and you here in the Philippines can be part of it. The time is now!"

Over a decade ago, Morris had planted thousands of spiritual seeds in the Philippines by providing instructions for nationals on how to hold their own crusades. Through this program around the world, nearly two million people received Jesus as Savior and more than three thousand new churches were established.

To demonstrate the power of God as a proof producer,

Morris conducted the Manila Miracle Rally on May 3, 1984, in Luneta Park. In the afternoon before the rally, in a little over four hours, twelve inches of rain fell. Despite the rain, more than fifty thousand Filipinos showed up. Traffic was jammed for blocks with people in cars, buses and jitneys unable to reach the crusade grounds due to the storm.

Morris began to preach, as he often does, out of the 53rd chapter of Isaiah, the first six verses. "The most important thing for man to know is that God created this world," he began. "He created man, created him for a purpose. He created man, and even after man failed God in the Garden of Eden, God so loved him that He did not leave him in his sin, and did not leave him in his disobedience. God gave man a way out of the darkness. Jesus Christ came, and He paid the price, and now, all man has to do is to receive the work and the Son of God, the work that He did for them. Jesus atoned for your sins."

The crowd erupted in applause and excitement. When Morris invited these eager souls to accept Jesus Christ as their Savior, thousands of people lowered their umbrellas in the rain and raised their hands. Wheelchairs and crutches were passed to the platform in a mighty demonstration of the work of God's Spirit. Only eternity will reveal how many blind eyes were opened, how many crippled legs were made straight, and how many deaf ears first heard the name of Jesus.

At the miracle rally that night, as tears and raindrops ran down the faces of these precious Filipinos, they participated in a modern-day Philippine Pentecost. The impact of the violent demonstrations of the zealous New People's Army in that nation were dwarfed by the peaceful and life-giving Holy Spirit revolution of God's Victorious Army.

At the end of the School of Ministry meeting and the crusade, the Spirit of God spoke through the chosen warrior as he declared, "I will return to the Philippines on February 7, 1986."

At the time of this prophetic utterance, it could be known only by God that this was to be the week of crisis elections in the Philippines.

*   *   *

"Dear God, let it not be me," the reluctant Corazon Aquino prayed when she realized she was marked as the only person who could possibly defeat President Marcos. Only days after that prayerful petition, she was chosen as the opposition candidate.

On election day, February 7, 1986, President Marcos and his regime pushed Morris Cerullo World Evangelism's School of Ministry out of the P.I.C.C. hall previously reserved for the School of Ministry and put them instead into the large auditorium next door. The Holy Spirit knew that they would need this larger auditorium to facilitate the thousands of nationals that would be pouring into this destiny changing meeting.

While Morris was teaching thousands of pastors and young spiritual soldiers the principles of spiritual warfare on one side of the building, Marcos was trying to steal the election with fraudulent ballot counting on the other.

Marcos had allowed NAMFREL, an independent monitor, to tabulate election results in tandem with COMELEC, the official Commission on Elections. Marcos believed he could control the vote. He had decided to win by a credibly slim margin of victory instead of a suspicious landslide.

While NAMFREL reported Corazon ahead, COMELEC delayed the count to enable Marcos to tailor the total.

201

One night after the polls closed, thirty computer technicians counting the vote dramatized Marcos's sham by fleeing the COMELEC headquarters for the refuge of a church. They maintained that the figures showing Corazon in the lead were being destroyed.

Just over the wall were 4,200 national leaders representing all of the Philippine islands, interceding in prayer for God to move on behalf of their nation. Their plan of attack was to have God direct the outcome of this election not through vote counting, but by honoring the prayers of His God's Victorious Army soldiers.

Something historic was taking place at the Philippine International Convention Center in both the natural realm and the spiritual realm. One one side of the Philippine International Convention Center, there was a huge bank of computers tabulating the votes, which Marcos had schemed to counterfeit. But on the other side of the convention center, thousands of the nation's spiritual soldiers had gathered from all over the Philippines to learn spiritual warfare.

"Remember, the key to spiritual breakthrough is timing," the chosen warrior told his attentive troops. "In 1962, God spoke to me and said, 'Son, build me an Army.' At that moment God gave me the power to pass on His anointing to thousands of others, to share the New Testament miracle power with nationals all over the world. Every believer is a minister as he lays hold to the keys of the kingdom and begins to exercise the authority that is his through Jesus Christ the Messiah."

Morris taught them how to use front line spiritual warfare. He told them that the Philippines did not belong to the fraudulent government and the deceptive leaders who brought great suffering on humanity. The

Philippines, he declared, belonged to the children of the living God.

"This is your hour. This is not the hour of defeat. God has told me that Jesus is praying for the Philippines. What we face here as a challenge in the Philippine Islands, we face as a challenge in our world today. There is a great shaking coming—everything that can be shaken will be shaken: governments, economies, families, relationships, religious systems. And the shaking has started."

The prayers of these thousands of spiritual warriors set in motion God's divine power and authority. It would ultimately influence the outcome of this counterfeit election and help Aquino to receive victory.

Within two weeks, Marcos was out of Malacanang palace. God had moved miraculously to remove him from power without one ounce of bloodshed.

CHAPTER TWENTY-ONE

THE
HOPELESS
HIP

A single tear tricked down little Eduardo's cheek as he painfully hobbled down the dusty stairs outside his house.

Eduardo had learned the cruel lessons of pain sooner than most eight-year-old boys in Belo Horizonte, Brazil. A severe bone infection had eaten away a part of his hip, leaving a gaping hole and constant pain in his tiny body. Now he could do little more than sit on his front steps, watching his friends play soccer in the street in front of the house.

Eduardo had just heard about a miracle preacher named Morris Cerullo, who was coming from America. It was said that many people were healed at this preacher's miracle meetings. Eduardo wondered if he could be healed too.

"Mama, will you *pleeeeease* take me to the miracle meeting of this American preacher?" Eduardo hopefully asked his mother.

But Mrs. Serguera did not believe in miracles. She quickly brushed aside the pleading request of her hurting son.

"No, Eduardo, Mama's not going to take you to that meeting. I love you too much to see you get your hopes up for some sort of a silly miracle—then blam, get disappointed when nothing happens. No, Eduardo, it is best that you stay home and forget this miracle silliness."

Her sharp reply hurt Eduardo deep down in his gut. With his mother's few short sentences, it seemed that all his hope for a normal life, free of pain, was as shattered as his diseased hip. But in times of need, God often uses neighbors as His heavenly angels!

An Assembly of God church member who did believe in miracles had also heard about the miracle preacher.

She had also heard that Morris would be holding a big miracle meeting in Sao Paulo, which at the same time would be shown on a giant screen in Belo Horizonte. And she knew she must somehow take her neighbor boy, Eduardo Serguera, to that miracle meeting to ask God for his healing.

So it was that on June 23, 1984, when Morris Cerullo instructed the sick people in Sao Paulo to put their hands on the area of their sickness, little Eduardo heard Morris Cerullo's voice and saw the preacher's determined face on the large screen in Belo Horizonte. And he put his hand on his right leg, near his hip.

"Take my brace off," Eduardo said after his childlike prayer to the heavenly Father. "I felt something tingly happen in my body. I believe God has done something to my hip."

As soon as the brace was off, Eduardo stood up and started to walk without his constant childhood companion. And he immediately knew in his heart that he would be able to run perfectly without his crutches! The pain was instantly gone. Eduardo was able to run, jump and play like any other normal eight-year-old boy. He wasn't crippled anymore. The Spirit of God had touched and miraculously healed that little boy.

On that memorable June 23, Morris Cerullo took that same saving and healing message of Jesus Christ that Eduardo experienced to hundreds of thousands of men, women, boys and girls across Brazil, North America, and Asia—all at the same time!

On June 23, 1984, Morris Cerullo personally conducted a great miracle healing crusade rally, a Day of Miracles, in Sao Paulo, Brazil. All the events that transpired at that great miracle rally were captured by video cameras and transmitted almost instantly by microwave and international satellite technology to large screens in eight other cities in Brazil and in sixty North American cities, and to a potential television viewing audience of seven million people in Hong Kong and China.

The sophisticated communications equipment flawlessly picked up the entire rally and beamed it out across the jungles of Brazil to Rio de Janeiro, to Belo Horizonte, to Belem, and to five more cities. The Word went out to thousands of needy Brazilian people.

The equipment also beamed the same Day of Miracles and One Million Soul Crusade out across the Caribbean, across the Gulf of Mexico, and into the awaiting auditoriums, arenas and ballrooms of North America.

And halfway around the world, excited television viewers in Hong Kong and China witnessed the historic rally as well.

In just one night at least 125,835 souls gave their lives to Jesus and were saved from those fiery pits of hell that God had allowed Morris Cerullo to see vividly as a young boy.

In just one week more than fifteen thousand Brazilian pastors and lay leaders were simultaneously trained in a School of Ministry originating in Sao Paulo and transmitted by microwave to eight other cities.

In just one outreach more Brazilian nationals were trained in the week-long School of Ministry than could have ever been trained by conventional means.

On June 23, 1984, on the Day of Miracles, God had touched Eduardo, one little crippled boy. He also touched the entire nation of Brazil and the world. Through the death and resurrection of Jesus Christ, God provided for the salvation and healing of millions of Brazilian souls like Eduardo. June 23, 1984, is a date that will forever remain meaningful to little Eduardo. And June 23, 1984, is a date that would become a milestone in Christian history.

The following documents underscore the historic significance of the event:

• Jerry Patton, multi-media expert, recalls the Day of Miracles:

"To link sixty cities in North America, nine cities in Brazil, and millions of television viewers in Asia through complicated satellite and microwave technology was a gigantic and unprecedented task.

"Nothing quite like this Morris Cerullo outreach had ever been done before in the history of Christianity.

"Just getting the equipment together that was needed to produce the Day of Miracles crusade in Brazil was a major project. We needed three complete air cargo containers to ship it (and that does not include the myriad of equipment that we rented in Brazil).

"Every piece of audio and video equipment had to be painstakingly cleared and itemized for customs in both English and Portuguese; the customs documents were nineteen pages long.

"Part of the equipment list included thirty Bose 802 speakers, eighteen 10' x 14' screens, and eighteen Barco video projections, plus thousands of feet of camera cable and microphone wire, seven video cameras and spare parts for the machines.

"Electronic, audio, lighting, video, satellite and micro-wave technologies are all challenges in themselves, but when they are combined with cultural differences and language barriers, the task of putting on the Day of Miracles seemed to be nearly impossible without the grace of a loving and compassionate God.

"God brought us just the right people to do the task.

"A crew of twenty-four highly trained computer and satellite technicians from the United States ventured to Brazil to assist Morris Cerullo World Evangelism's own technicians in this historic outreach.

"In each city, local convention centers were rented. Those locations with too much light for daytime viewing of the School of Ministry had their windows darkened by a deep black plastic covering for the program.

"To publicize this historic Day of Miracles rally, six Portuguese television programs were created using some of the best footage of Morris Cerullo ministering in Schools of Ministry and crusades."

• "How Would Brazilians React to the Large Screen?" by the Staff Satellite Coordinator

"My task was to bring the School of Ministry from Sao Paulo, Brazil, to the eight different locations in Brazil by using microwave and satellite technology.

"In each city, our plan was to project the images originated in Sao Paulo onto large screens in eight different cities so that thousands of other Brazilian pastors and lay people could watch the School of Ministry, and then the Day of Miracles crusade, just as though Morris Cerullo were actually preaching under God's anointing in their own hometown.

"In Brazil, most churches do not allow their congregations to even own television sets or to go to the movies.

"How would the Brazilian students react to a large screen?

"Would the pastors even allow their cautious congregations to participate in this media event that was so similar to television and movies?

"Brazilian Christians are conservative in their dress, and very reserved in their worship.

"There is little clapping or active participation in the services.

"How would these highly traditional Brazilian Christians actually receive Morris Cerullo's highly untraditional messages?

"Would they actually respond and attempt to participate in the miracle services at their individual School of Ministry locations?

"I did not have to wait very long for my answers.

"Only minutes after Morris Cerullo started preaching, the over two thousand delegate students in the Sao Paulo site were responding to his message with totally untraditional, enthusiastic clapping and praise.

"But more significantly, from every large-screen location in Brazil the reports were universal: The pastors and students are all clapping and praising as though Morris Cerullo were here in person!

"Breakthroughs.

"That's what our outreach in Brazil was all about.

"We told the people of Brazil that Morris Cerullo is a man with a message from God. In their deep and trusting faith, these Brazilians came expecting to hear an anointed message from God.

"With tears running down my eyes, I can tell you they were not disappointed.

"God spoke, and Brazil will never be the same!

• An Open Letter to Morris Cerullo, by Adelson Da Silva, Belem, Brazil

"Since my being in the Brazilian School of Ministry, my life is really changed. I really do feel the responsibility and call that I have received from the Lord.

"Now I am no longer a sergeant in the Brazilian army, I am a soldier in the army of Christ!

"God has already told me, through prophecy and His Word, that He has a work for me to do in His harvest field.

"The School of Ministry gave me the spiritual tools to accomplish what I must do for God.

"I am most grateful to God and to Morris Cerullo for this most valuable ministry.

"My prayer is that God will continue to use you and your staff in this great work of organizing God's Victorious Army."

People called by God to help others find salvation in Christ must have faith for their own families too. Morris Cerullo is no exception, as we will see in the next chapter.

CHAPTER TWENTY-TWO

THE FINAL STRATEGY

On August 10, 1985, the hall of Atlanta's World Congress Center was packed to capacity by nearly eighteen hundred Christians from the United States and ten other nations.

They had convened with Morris Cerullo to launch one of the most historic outreaches in the history of Christianity—the Global Satellite Network. The Global Satellite Network represents the fulfillment of a vision, a methodology to establish an ongoing presence in the nations of the world, teaching, equipping and mobilizing foreign nationals to reach their own nations. The purpose of the Global Satellite Network is to communicate on a monthly basis with nationals around the world, training, equipping, mobilizing and then sending them as proof producers to witness the power of Jesus Christ in their own cities and nations.

Culminating decades of frontline evangelism by Morris Cerullo, the launching of the Global Satellite Network enabled him to reach the world by using the most modern technology known to humans.

"Our God-given idea is to have this powerful satellite

uplink/downlink on a monthly basis to hundreds of United States and foreign sites around the world," Morris Cerullo announced to the crowd. The atmosphere was electric.

While the satellites beamed his message to a multitude of locations, Morris Cerullo taught and demonstrated his New Anointing message step by step to the enthusiastic audience in Atlanta and to the equally enthusiastic audiences in other key locations.

"It is like liquid fire all over this building," he said, describing the powerful outpouring of the Holy Spirit.

The students sitting under this teaching did not know that Morris had spent the past week in prayer and fasting for this historic event. The evidence of this warrior's diligent preparation for this mighty spiritual battle was in the powerful presence of God that permeated the building and in the anointing upon his words.

The School of Ministry students had come to Atlanta and to the other satellite locations to be trained on how to be used by God as an instrument of His power. To become proof producers. To demonstrate God's power on earth to others.

They were not taught simply a theory or theology. They personally experienced God's power and anointing in their own lives. Pastors from many denominations came and their ministries were revolutionized.

Others came seeking answers to their physical, mental and emotional problems. Parents came searching for help in desperate family situations. Others had strong physical needs, or were desperately seeking relief from spiritual oppression.

No one was disappointed.

Answers came.

Healings happened.

Marriages were rekindled.

Spiritual victories were everywhere.

All received a new divine power: the New Anointing power of God!

With tears flowing down his cheeks, Morris declared, "The power of God is flowing in this building like a mighty river."

The deep compassion of this unique, endtime prophet was much in evidence. Many times he stopped the meeting to soak in what the Holy Spirit was doing in the audience.

"What time is it?" he asked.

"It's Harvest Time!" was the unanimous reply.

These well-trained soldiers for God know they are living in the closing years of spiritual history and that Jesus is coming soon.

The little Jewish preacher then continued, "Devil, you stay on your side of the line. You are already defeated. God has already defeated the devil. Do not look to your future in defeat, but look to your future as bright, for God will carry you on from victory to victory, from faith to faith, from power to power, to conquer all the power of the devil."

The audience erupted into praise and worship.

When the room was once again quiet, Morris continued. "I want to make a prophecy here tonight. I prophesy to you that God is going to call Himself out a people. The chains of denominationalism are going to break and the body of Christ is going to be united, not in heaven but here on earth, in the name of Jesus."

Morris wept openly.

"You and I are chosen and ordained by God for a divine purpose. There is no total victory until we learn to conquer an enemy that is already defeated! You need a spiritual breakthrough. My prayer is that God will grant to you the anointing of the Holy Spirit so you can see God as He really is, so you will not limit our unlimited God!"

Once again, the crowd erupted in praise, worship and clapping. The love of God and His presence poured out over the entire auditorium.

Throughout his life of ministry since 1962, over five hundred thousand men and women have been personally trained by Morris Cerullo to go forth as proof producers in their nations. But the chosen warrior knew even that mighty effort was not enough! That's why he launched the Global Satellite Network on this day—to multiply himself by the power of the media so he could train and anoint even more nationals to reach their nations for Jesus Christ.

*   *   *

- Seven thousand islands.
- Sixty million people.
- Fifty-nine different dialects.
- Hindered by ancient methods of inter-island transportation and communication.
- Crippled by political upheavals.
- Disrupted by aggressive communism, powered by the young and well-armed New People's Army.

These are just some of the divergent and challenging factors in the Philippines that make a ministry outreach to this nation seem impossible.

But in January, 1989—a critical year in God's dealing with His Chosen Warrior Morris Cerullo—the Lord gave His servant his most significant spiritual challenge.

At the 1989 Morris Cerullo World Conference, he announced to the nations of the world that: "God has given me a divine mandate to reach one billion souls for His glory before the year 2000."

As he spoke to an audience of thousands who were deeply touched and inspired by the magnitude of that mandate, Morris revealed his inspired World-Wide Outreach Plan to reach *all* the other nations of the world—to reach one billion souls before the year 2000!

"God has challenged you and me to build a billion-soul army," he continued, "and He has given us a seven-point master ministry plan to achieve His purpose. The key elements He has shown me in this divinely inspired plan can be briefly summarized in seven steps:

"1. We must demonstrate to the nations of the world the need to come together in spiritual unity. Unity in the spirit will give the Body of Christ an unparalleled strength in this endtime hour.

"2. God has told me He is going to bestow a new mantle of spiritual power and authority on dedicated foreign nationals and other key apostolic leaders who are willing to give up everything they have and yield themselves totally to His Will for the cause of Christ.

"3. We must continue and intensify our training of the foreign nationals."

Morris understood the vital importance of this step, so he paused for a bit to let his words sink into this dedicated gathering before he continued.

"We must be prepared to let them take back the Morris Cerullo Schools of Ministry to their local areas so they can train other ministers and workers in the proof producers' style, teaching them the answer to the question, 'What must we do that we might work the works of God?'

"4. We must demonstrate to these foreign nationals how they can mobilize huge crowds and conduct mass evangelistic crusades so they can act as God's vessels for the miracle of salvation and healing."

When Morris announced this point, many of the nationals in the audience stood and cheered loudly, knowing full well how beneficial it would be to their ministries to be shown personally by him how to mobilize and conduct crusades.

"5. We must teach them how to use the latest micro-wave and satellite and television technology to bring the Morris Cerullo Global Satellite Network to their own local area on a monthly basis. Only through continued, monthly training can they be properly prepared for the endtime spiritual battles that lie ahead.

"6. It is up to us to demonstrate how to move into television and radio with the gospel. The foreign nationals must learn how to use the media to multiply their outreach to the unsaved and lost."

Before Morris revealed the seventh point, he paused, waiting for absolute silence so the full impact of this last nation-changing point could permeate every part of their spirits.

"7. We must place the vital weapons of spiritual war-fare into their hands, for the weapons of warfare are not carnal, but spiritual!

"We must give them the key ministry books, the monthly Victory Miracle Library, the video and audio tapes of various Schools of Ministry—all the tools God has given us to help build Him an invincible army!"

The conference erupted into praise, worship, and thanksgiving as Morris Cerullo finished outlining God's master plan for **one billion souls!**

Everyone present at the conference sensed in their spirits the magnitude of this mighty mandate to reach one billion souls. The year 1989 would be forever etched in their minds as perhaps the most spiritually significant in the history of this chosen warrior's ministry.

1989 revealed the ministry theme, the plan, and the purpose that would propel Morris Cerullo World Evangelism through the last decade of the twentieth century, a decade of destiny.

For in 1989, God clearly spoke to Morris Cerullo and gave him the divinely-authored mandate to bring the gospel to the world, revealing to him the global strategy and technology needed to reach one billion souls for Jesus Christ before the year 2000!

*   *   *

In the far north of the Philippine islands, in the sin-hardened oil-drilling district of Cebu City, a very gentle, petite woman is quietly going about her work, impacting her nation for Jesus Christ.

Det Sayson is a lay leader who has put her life down on the altar to be used by God as a handmaiden of the Lord to reach her nation as the Global Satellite Director in the Philippines for Morris Cerullo World Evangelism.

"Twelve Global Satellite Sites are not enough," she tells the ministers in her meeting.

"To reach the Philippines, we must intensify our efforts. I believe we should have twenty sites by the end of the year!"

The ministers marvel at the boldness and the determination of this woman. But they listen, because they know her story. They know she has personally ventured into the Philippines worst prisons. They know that God has used her to produce life-changing miracles in the lives of the worst of murderers, thieves, rapists and every other kind of criminal.

They know that she unceasingly travels the islands with her portable satellite equipment by jeep, by boat, by van, and by foot to train nationals who cannot be reached any other way.

From fifty to three thousand Filipinos come once a month to each site to hear the Word and be equipped through the Morris Cerullo Global Satellite Network. They know that these same Morris Cerullo School of Ministry principles of demonstrating the power of God through signs and wonders have helped Reverend Eddie Villanueva in Manila to lead a powerful church that meets each Sunday in an open school courtyard with a congregation of over twenty-five thousand people at a time.

So they listen to Det Sayson as she declares:

"The Morris Cerullo Global Satellite Network is how God's Victorious Army is going to reach the Philippines and a billion souls in our world for Christ by training nationals and by unifying the body of Christ!"

Det paused for a deep breath, then continued.

"It is time to beat the devil in his own playground. We must rise up together, rise up and establish more sites for the Morris Cerullo Global Satellite Network to reach and train the nationals on these seven thousand islands.

"Bullets will not stop communism...only the blood of Jesus.

"Politics will not save the Philippines. Only on-fire, dedicated proof producers, who can demonstrate the power of God to the people in their own province.

"Economic reform will not change our existence. Only a nation of dedicated, on-fire, born-again Christians with high moral standards will reverse the economic corruption in our country."

Her exhortations continued for another hour. At the end of her message, the seeds for a new satellite site had been sown. As she went back to her lonely, simple room that night, Det Sayson climbed into bed with a tear in her eye.

"Oh Lord," she prayed, "I'm very tired. The intense travel sometimes is more than I can bear. Please give me Your divine strength to continue this ministry. Please give me Your divine wisdom and guidance to know where to go and what to say. And finally, dear Lord, please help me, just as your chosen warrior Morris Cerullo has taught me, to pass the anointing and the burden you have given to me on to others. Amen."

In the quiet of the night, as Det's fatigued body melts into the flimsy mattress, she knows in her spirit that God is already restoring her strength for tomorrow's new battle on the frontlines of God's Victorious Army.

*　　　　*　　　　*

"I am hereby declaring war on the devil's war," the chosen warrior proclaimed. "God has given us new marching orders," he continued, "telling us to go on the attack against Satan's army of the ungodly. We must wake up and mobilize the slumbering army of God and move forward against the devil's twin lieutenants of despair and disease.

We're going into battle with Almighty God's biggest guns: hope and healing. We must demonstrate firsthand what God is doing. "I believe God wants me to prod and poke the body of Christ in North America from a pudgy, couch-potato spiritual life-style to fitness for battle."

The spiritual commander-in-chief stood steadfast, addressing his attentive troops throughout the entire nation in a strong, confident, yet compassionate manner.

"This is a whole new truth for all of God's Army for the decade of the 1990's. I am calling up the reserves for training to go out and meet the devil on what he thinks is his territory, and beat his ears back!

"I believe that we will see tens and hundreds of thousands at a time coming into the kingdom as the result of seeing and hearing for themselves how God can supernaturally work life-changing miracles at the hands of His obedient people."

Knowing that the church of Jesus Christ has been for far too long divided into squabbling segments, the chosen warrior then called for division and strife to stop.

"God is calling us all to be unified in this new era of soul winning...the Pentecostals...the Baptists...the Episcopalians...the whole body of Christ is being called and challenged to build up believers and to minister to and meet the needs of God's people. This can only happen as we are prepared to become proof producers and allow God to work miracles and demonstrate His power in us and through us."

After forty-two years of ministering to the nations of the world; after God guiding his life in every phase—from the days as a little Jewish orphan to his days as an international evangelist—God has been preparing Morris Cerullo for this moment and this incredible spiritual challenge: to reach one billion souls before the year 2000.

And God's Victorious Army is prepared.

Morris Cerullo's burden for the nationals is greater now than ever before..."the foreign national is **the key** to reaching the nations for God."

"The unbeliever will feel the convicting power of the Holy Spirit drawing him to God," Morris explains, "as only the unvarnished truth about Satan and his plans becomes evident." Through the proof producing power of God the sinner receives the greatest miracle in the world—the miracle of salvation. Then the sick are made whole and the people know that God really cares about them.

*   *   *

On that quiet day in October of 1931, no one could sense any historical significance to the birth of Moshe (Moses) Cerullo.

Not Mama Bertha.

Not Papa Joseph.

Not the local rabbi.

But in the decades since that day, as the life of Morris Cerullo has unfolded, it is clear that this chosen warrior has significantly affected the spiritual destiny of the Jews and of the nations of the world.

The day is not yet done for this chosen warrior.

There are battles left to fight.

Over 3.3 billion people have never heard the name of Jesus Christ even once. He has been commissioned by God to reach at least one billion souls before the year 2000.

The storybook ending says that old soldiers never die, they just fade away into the time-worn glories of battles long ago fought. But this is real life and this fiery general in God's Army has no time to meditate on past victories.

With each spiritual enemy encounter, Morris Cerullo grows stronger. He continues to radiate a spiritual explosion of God's proof producing power, walking in signs and wonders to wake up a slumbering world that is fading fast into the seductive fires of hell.

As the sun fades over the mountain at the end of the day, and darkness sets upon the earth, the voice of the chosen warrior can be heard above the sleeping earth, talking to his God in fervent prayer, saying:

"Lord, continue to give me the strength, the wisdom, the anointing, and Your proof-producing power, so that I fulfill your mandate and reach one billion souls for Your Glory before the year 2000."